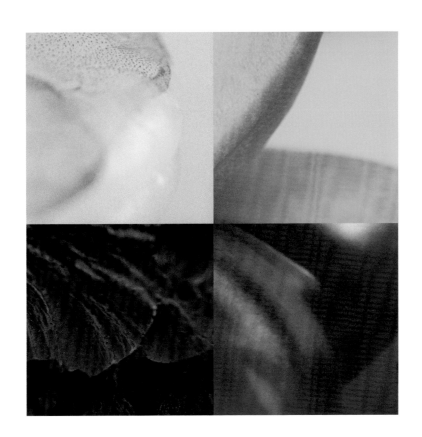

STAR PALATE

CELEBRITY COOKBOOK FOR A CURE

Tami Agassi & Kathy Casey

Documentary Media
Seattle, Washington

Star Palate: Celebrity Cookbook for a Cure

© 2004 Marsha Rivkin Center for Ovarian Cancer Research

Published in 2004 by

Documentary Media

3250 41st Ave SW

Seattle WA 98116

books@docbooks.com

www.documentarymedia.com

(206) 935-9292

Printed in Canada

Authors: Tami Agassi and Kathy Casey

Recipe Development and Testing: Kathy Casey Food Studios

Managing Editor: Petyr Beck, Documentary Media

Editor: Judy Gouldthorpe

Food Photography: David Bell, Studio 3

Food Stylist: Christine Jackson

Additional Photography: Marc Carter, Tami Agassi

Book Design: The Red Army Creative

Publisher: Barry Provorse, Documentary Media

"Kathy Casey Food Studios" and "Dish D'Lish" are registered trademarks of Kathy Casey, Inc.

Library of Congress Cataloging-in-Publication Data

Agassi, Tami,

Star palate: celebrity cookbook for a cure / [compiled] by Tami Agassi & Kathy Casey; foreword by Libby Gates Armintrout.—1st ed.

p. cm.

Includes index.

ISBN 0-9719084-5-1

1. Cookery. I. Casey, Kathy. II. Title.

TX714.A4235 2004

641.5—dc22

2004009763

TABLE OF CONTENTS

Dedication   7

Foreword   8

Introduction   10

Starters & Drinks   12

Soups & Salads   32

Main Courses   54

Pasta & Risotto   80

Comforts, Snacks & Favorites   98

Sides, Accompaniments & Breakfast   122

Sweets, Desserts & Other Indulgences   144

Things You Should Know   165

Index   166

Beneficiaries   170

Special Thanks   172

Credits   175

Marsha Rivkin   Revella Bensussen

DEDICATION

This book is dedicated in loving memory to Revella Bensussen and

Marsha Rivkin, two women of valor who nourished their families

with tremendous love. Although their lives were short, they continue

to inspire. As angels above, they guide us through our fight to find a

cure. We love you, we miss you, and we honor your memory always.

FOREWORD

The Gates family, Christmas 1972 (pictured clockwise from top left): Bill, Bill Sr., Libby, Mary, and Kristi.

So many of my fondest family memories are wrapped around family meals, I find it impossible to separate the idea of a wonderful meal from community. Family is the first and most basic community in society, and in our family one of the most powerful "community-building" times occurred around the dinner table each night. This loving link between conversation and nourishment was a consistent part of growing up for me and my siblings. My dad sat at one end and my mother at the other, and we used the dinner table to share the things that had happened during the day.

My mother had many interests and far-reaching responsibilities as a University of Washington regent, a member of corporate boards, and a committed community volunteer. My brother, sister, and I listened to our parents talk at the table about shared accomplishments, professional dilemmas, and community service.

Now that my mother is gone, we still miss her when the rest of us slip back into our same places when we gather at Dad's for meals. Now, I try to build community at my own home, too, where my family makes a big effort to have dinner together.

A tantalizing meal for the Gates family is what's called "comfort" food today. It includes meat and potatoes served with my maternal grandmother's gravy and, for dessert, ice cream with her "sticky" chocolate sauce, neither of which has ever been duplicated to our satisfaction. Though my brother has the opportunity to experience a global palate, it's the old family recipes he most enjoys: clam chowder, tuna casserole, apple pie, and, of course, hamburgers.

Comfort was not the only emotion experienced at our table. The Gates family is a little competitive. At our family getaway on Washington State's beautiful Hood Canal, where we had time to prepare meals and have wonderful conversations in the kitchen, dinner was always followed by cutthroat card games to see who had to do the dishes.

One of my memories is the image of my brother reading the Economist at the dinner table and his having to be pulled away to blow out his birthday candles. What a relief it was for my unsuspecting mom and dad to know that the "argumentative little boy" they faced each night at dinner would finally turn into something.

When my mother became ill with breast cancer, the bedside became the focus of our family's life. When the rest of us sat for dinner, we made sure that she could continue participating in our conversations.

That's why the idea of a cookbook is so appealing to me. So much community building happens around a joyous meal, just as it does when someone is suffering. Whether we're opening our homes to friends for entertainment or caring for someone who is unwell, we extend ourselves to nourish others. One of the gestures we appreciated most when my mother was dying was the subtle delivery of meals to our doorstep by caring people in our community.

My brother and his wife are committed to improving the condition of world health through the Bill & Melinda Gates Foundation, and he has taken a personal interest in research related to finding cures, which for many diseases are almost in our grasp. My dad sits at the head of the table there, too, as co-chair of the foundation.

The dedication of caring people is important to these causes and funding is, too. I think it's wonderful that celebrities have taken the time to share their favorite recipes to support two important women's health issues, breast and ovarian cancer.

The sharing of a personal recipe is a heartfelt gift, and that's what makes this book so special. It is my hope that Star Palate will assist in elevating our awareness not only of the threat of breast and ovarian cancer, but also of the possibility of a cure. When that day comes, we'll all have reason to celebrate, and what better way to do it than with a scrumptious meal with family and friends.

—Libby Gates Armintrout

INTRODUCTION

This collection of recipes isn't just a pretty coffee-table book—it's a culinary adventure that home chefs will actually enjoy without intimidation. If Tami Agassi and Kathy Casey ever visit your home, they want to see this book in the kitchen with dog-eared pages, grimy, splattered, and stained with use. This is a book meant to be well loved with dirty fingerprints and smudges.

The *Star Palate* cookbook concept was dreamed up by Tami during her own treatment for cancer. She and her good friend Gloria Bensussen began the long hours and hard work to make this book a reality.

It seemed natural to create a celebrity cookbook as a fundraiser because food is such an integral part of every person's life. After all, everybody has a favorite celeb and they have to eat, too! Most people are curious as to what the "elite" are wearing, who they're marrying and divorcing, but rarely does one hear about what they cook up for themselves when the cameras are off. So why not take a sneak peek into what your favorite celebs are eating these days?

Tami and Gloria realized that without a cooking authority on board, writing a cookbook would be like trying to reinvent the wheel! Therefore, the help of chef and author Kathy Casey was solicited. Now that the ball was rolling, it was time to get recipes from famous celebrities and world-renowned chefs.

Asking a celebrity for an autograph is daunting enough, let alone asking them to submit a recipe! It was Tami's job to get the recipes in some shape or form, whether it be chicken scratch or photocopy, then Kathy's job to test and rewrite them for the home cook. When the recipes came in, they ran the gamut. Some contained detailed explanations, while a few were annotated with illegible markings. Many represented cherished childhood memories or old family favorites and traditions passed on. Others were creations cooked with friends or dishes created by favorite chefs. Some of the recipes were in great "culinary shape" and others needed some interpretation. The goal was to make each recipe user-friendly for all home cooks in their own kitchens.

This is a book in which food is as important as the stars themselves, so it had to look great. The well-tested recipes went from Kathy Casey Food Studios to the photographer's studio, where one by one the dishes were photographed. Lights! Camera! Styling! With careful attention to detail, the food could be photographed without "makeup" or touch-ups.

Inspired by the desire to raise awareness of and funds for breast and ovarian cancer research, the end result is a collection of fun and delicious recipes with worldwide origins. Kathy and Tami are delighted to share this book with you, and their wish is for your favorite star's recipe to become a favorite that you can share with family and friends. By doing so, you are helping in the effort to find a cure for breast and ovarian cancer.

STARTERS & DRINKS

At any good gathering, party, or soirée, appetizers and cocktails can set the mood for a delicious meal or even be the meal. As dining trends change, small plates are becoming more popular. With appetizers, the home chef has an opportunity to get creative and make a WOW! first impression. And what you sip while you nibble is just as important. Cocktails have become as creative an outlet as their appetizer counterparts. So pick a few recipes, choose a libation, call some friends, and let the conversation flow!

Uncle Louie's Chicken Wings Marinara—Jay Leno   14

Fiesta Shrimp Cocktail—Chef Sheila Lukins   16

Fragrant Lamb-Stuffed Vine Leaves—Celine Dion   18

Mandarin Star—Chef Kathy Casey   20

Tuna Pizza—Iron Chef Masaharu Morimoto   22

Green Juice—Donna Karan   24

Wontons in Hot-and-Sour Chili Sauce—Chef Martin Yan   26

Rosemary Parmesan Puffs—Chef Kathy Casey   28

Watermelon Twist—Liz Smith   30

Makes 24 pieces

1 dozen chicken wings or 2 dozen drumettes

2 tablespoons olive oil

1 tablespoon garlic powder or granulated garlic

1 teaspoon salt

½ teaspoon black pepper

1 cup marinara sauce

2 tablespoons Durkee Hot Sauce, or to taste

4 garlic cloves, chopped

Chopped fresh parsley, for garnish

Jay Leno is a comedian, actor, and NBC's Tonight Show *host.*

JAY LENO

UNCLE LOUIE'S CHICKEN WINGS MARINARA

Wing lovers will be jaywalking to your house for these! The recipe multiplies easily for a party—just be sure to use extra pans as needed so as not to crowd the wings while roasting. For extra mouthwatering goodness, serve a Gorgonzola dip along with the marinara sauce.

Preheat oven to 400°F.

If using whole wings, disjoint wings and remove tips; you should have 24 drumettes.

In a large bowl, toss the chicken with oil, garlic powder, salt, and pepper. Arrange on a rack in a baking pan. Roast chicken in preheated oven until done, about 30 minutes.

Meanwhile, place the marinara sauce, hot sauce, and raw garlic in a blender and blend to purée garlic. When wings are done, remove from the oven, and toss wings with half the sauce. Leave oven on. Return wings to oven for 10 minutes more.

Sprinkle the wings with parsley. Serve with the remaining sauce on the side to dip the wings into.

Sheila Lukins is a chef, food writer, and author of the award-winning, best-selling cookbook The Silver Palate. *She has been Food Editor for* Parade *magazine since 1986.*

CHEF SHEILA LUKINS
FIESTA SHRIMP COCKTAIL

This refreshing combination of flavors is festive in both appearance and taste.

In a medium saucepan, combine water, wine, celery, parsley, and peppercorns. Bring to a boil over medium-high heat. Add the shrimp. Cover and simmer until cooked through (the shrimp will turn pink), about 2 minutes. Drain, run under cold water, and drain well again. Refrigerate until chilled.

To make the salsa: Using a rubber spatula, combine the papaya, tomato, cucumber, red onion, lime juice, jalapeño, and oil in a large bowl. Season with salt and pepper to taste. Fold in the chopped mint.

To serve, place 5 shrimp in the bottom of each of 4 martini glasses. Top each with ½ cup of the salsa. Place 3 shrimp, grouped together, on the rim of each glass. Garnish with mint sprigs.

Makes 4 servings

1 cup water

½ cup dry white wine

2 stalks celery with leaves, chopped

4 sprigs parsley

4 black peppercorns

1 ½ to 2 pounds large shrimp, peeled and deveined (you need 32 shrimp)

4 large sprigs fresh mint, for garnish

Salsa

1 ripe papaya, halved, seeded, peeled and cut into ½-inch pieces

1 cup ½-inch-diced, seeded ripe tomato

½ cup ½-inch-diced, peeled seedless cucumber

¼ cup ¼-inch-diced red onion

2 tablespoons fresh lime juice

1 teaspoon very finely minced jalapeño

1 tablespoon olive oil

Salt and freshly ground black pepper

6 tablespoons coarsely chopped fresh mint leaves

CELINE DION
FRAGRANT LAMB-STUFFED VINE LEAVES

Makes about 30 pieces

2 8-ounce jars grape leaves, such as Orlando California grape leaves

½ cup long-grain rice

3 cups water

¼ cup plus 2 teaspoons olive oil

1 onion, finely chopped

½ pound ground lamb

5 tablespoons fresh lemon juice, divided

1 egg

¼ cup finely chopped Italian parsley

2 tablespoons finely chopped fresh mint

½ teaspoon dried oregano

½ teaspoon ground turmeric

½ teaspoon ground black pepper

¼ teaspoon ground white pepper

¼ teaspoon ground cardamom

¼ teaspoon ground nutmeg

¼ teaspoon ground cinnamon

⅛ teaspoon ground cloves

1 teaspoon salt

1 teaspoon finely chopped garlic

¼ cup water

Famed singer and performer Celine Dion flavors these with a special Arabian pepper seasoning, made of finely milled white and black pepper, cardamom, nutmeg, 4-spices, clove, and cinnamon. If you can find it, you can use it in place of the seasonings given in the recipe. You can also serve these with tahini sauce for dipping.

Put grape leaves in a big bowl and cover with boiling water. Let stand for 20 minutes, then rinse and drain well. Separate leaves and put them on a clean white towel. Reserve any broken ones for lining the pan.

Meanwhile, make the stuffing: Place rice and 3 cups water in a saucepan. Bring to a boil and cook rice for 5 minutes; drain.

In a nonstick skillet, heat ¼ cup oil and sauté onion for about 10 minutes. Add lamb and cook well. Add rice, 3 tablespoons lemon juice, egg, and seasonings.

Spread out 30 grape leaves, cutting off the hard stems. Put a rounded tablespoon of stuffing on each leaf, and roll carefully, tucking the sides so the stuffing will be secured. You now have 30 little packages.

Line a big pot with 10 grape leaves. Add the 30 rolls, seam at the bottom. Rolls should fit tightly. Add garlic, 2 teaspoons olive oil, 2 tablespoons lemon juice, and ¼ cup water. Cover with remaining grape leaves. Place a plate on top to secure everything.

Bring to a boil, then reduce heat and simmer, covered, for about 50 minutes. Uncover and let stand for a while.

Put on a serving dish and serve at room temperature.

"It was with great emotion and a bit of nostalgia that I chose this recipe given to me by my mother-in-law. When I first met the Angelil family, I was mesmerized to see René's mother work so hard to prepare meals that were feasts for the palate. It was under her loving instruction that I learned how to make some of her son's favorite dishes." Celine Dion

CHEF KATHY CASEY
MANDARIN STAR

Cocktails are a classy addition to any party, get-together, or soirée. Creative sips are also a great conversation starter. Doyenne of drink and Seattle's culinary diva Kathy Casey shakes up this refreshing and inspired cocktail combination with a dash of cranberry and a sprig of rosemary for extra "herbaliciousness."

Makes 1 cocktail

1 sprig fresh rosemary

2 ounces (¼ cup) Absolut Mandarin vodka

1 ½ ounces (3 tablespoons) Dish D'Lish Lemon & Lime Sour Cocktailor™
or Homemade Sweet & Sour (recipe follows)

¼ ounce (1 ½ teaspoons) cranberry juice

1 slice star fruit, for garnish

Drop the rosemary sprig into a cocktail shaker, then fill with ice. Measure in the vodka, sour mix, and cranberry juice.

Cap with shaker can and shake vigorously. Strain into a chilled martini glass.

Cut a slit partway through the star fruit slice and place on rim of glass for garnish.

Homemade Sweet & Sour

Makes 2 cups

½ cup fresh lime juice

½ cup fresh lemon juice

1 cup simple syrup*

In a large jar with a lid, combine ingredients. Cover and keep refrigerated for up to 2 weeks, or freeze.

*Simple syrup is available at bar supply stores. Or, to make it, combine 4 cups sugar and 1 quart water in a heavy pan. Bring to a boil, stirring to dissolve the sugar. Boil for 2 minutes. Remove from heat and let cool. Bottle and store at room temperature until needed. Keeps indefinitely.

"I created this cocktail especially for this book. It is the signature drink for the Star Palate galas. It could be the star of your next gala, too." Kathy Casey, NW celebrity chef, owner of Kathy Casey Food Studios & Dish D'Lish, author and TV personality

"Cooking is entertainment," says TV's Iron Chef Morimoto. You are certain to be entertained in his Philadelphia eatery, Morimoto Restaurant.

**Makes 1 small pizza,
serving 2 to 4 as an appetizer**

1 8-inch flour tortilla

Eel sauce or thickened (reduced) teriyaki sauce for brushing*

5 ounces sashimi-grade blue fin tuna, thinly sliced into 12 pieces

5 paper-thin (1/16- to 1/8-inch) slices red onion

6 very thin slices Roma tomato

6 very thin slices jalapeño pepper

1 tablespoon mayonnaise

1/4 teaspoon anchovy paste

Tabasco, if desired

Fresh cilantro leaves

IRON CHEF MASAHARU MORIMOTO
TUNA PIZZA

Chef Morimoto's swanky twist on pizza is a perfect starter to any dinner party or summer soirée.

Heat the grill. Grill tortilla on one side, then turn over and brush tortilla with eel sauce. Grill other side until crispy.

Lay tortilla, sauce side up, on a cutting board, and place the tuna on tortilla, covering the shell. Spread onions over tuna. Arrange tomatoes on top of onions, and place a jalapeño slice on each tomato slice. Cut pizza into 6 pieces and transfer to a plate.

Mix mayonnaise and anchovy paste, then decoratively dollop slices with a little of the sauce. If desired, place 1 drop Tabasco on each jalapeño slice. Place cilantro on center of each slice.

*Eel sauce is available at stores that are well stocked with Japanese food products.

Makes 1 to 2 servings

3 organic apples

1 stalk celery

1 cup spinach leaves or kale

1-inch piece fresh ginger

½ fennel bulb

½ cup parsley

½ cucumber

Add-ins:

1 tablespoon tocotrienols

1 tablespoon of your favorite nutrient/ mineral powder (Nature's First Food is a great one)

1 teaspoon goat's whey

1 teaspoon flaxseed oil

About 6 nuts (I prefer macadamias)

Fashion designer Donna Karan's Green Juice is as simple, sophisticated, and sensuous as her designs.

DONNA KARAN
GREEN JUICE

"A great way to start the day! Tocotrienols, powerful vitamin E derivatives, are antioxidants that have been shown to prevent cancer, lower cholesterol, and help maintain the health of your liver." Donna Karan

Pass the apples, celery, spinach, ginger, fennel, parsley, and cucumber through a juicer. Place mixture in a blender. Add the remaining ingredients. Blend, taking care to leave the nuts chunky so that you can chew them.

Serve immediately.

No one can dispute that Yan Can Cook. This chef, author, and culinary entertainer has been demonstrating his abilities for the last 18 years with his witty cooking series on PBS.

CHEF MARTIN YAN

WONTONS IN HOT-AND-SOUR CHILI SAUCE

Makes 4 first-course servings

Sauce

1 ½ tablespoons soy sauce

1 tablespoon seasoned rice vinegar

1 tablespoon Thai sweet chili sauce*

1 tablespoon minced green onion

1 teaspoon hot chili oil*

1 teaspoon minced cilantro

½ teaspoon minced garlic

¼ teaspoon minced ginger

Wontons

¼ pound ground pork

2 ounces uncooked shrimp, shelled, deveined, and finely chopped

1 egg white

1 teaspoon minced cilantro

½ teaspoon minced ginger

½ teaspoon sugar

½ teaspoon salt

⅛ teaspoon sesame oil

1/16 teaspoon ground white pepper

16 square wonton wrappers

Sliced green onion, for garnish

If you've never made wontons before, this is a good place to start—not only because the recipe is first-rate but also because the chef's instructions are thorough and easy to follow.

To make the sauce: Stir sauce ingredients together in a small bowl until blended. Reserve.

To make the wontons: Combine the ground pork, shrimp, egg white, cilantro, ginger, sugar, salt, sesame oil, and white pepper in a medium bowl, stirring rapidly with a fork in one direction until the mixture is stiff and spongy.

Place 1 heaping teaspoon of the filling in the center of each wonton wrapper. (Keep the remaining wrappers covered with a damp kitchen towel or plastic wrap to prevent them from drying out.) Brush the edges of the wrapper with a fingertip dipped in water, then fold the wrapper in half to form a triangle. Pinch the edges firmly to seal. Pull the opposite corners of the base of the triangle together, moisten one of the corners with water, and press the two base corners firmly together to seal. Cover the folded wontons with a damp kitchen towel to prevent drying. Repeat until all wontons are folded.

Bring a large pot of water to a boil. Slip the wontons into the water and bring the water back to a boil. Stir occasionally, especially when the wontons are first added, to prevent them from sticking to each other or the bottom of the pot. Cook until the wontons rise to the top of the water, about 5 minutes.

Scoop the wontons into a colander with a wire skimmer or slotted spoon, and drain. Toss the wontons and sauce together gently in a serving bowl until the wontons are lightly coated. Garnish with green onions if desired. Serve hot.

*Thai sweet chili sauce and hot chili oil are available at Asian markets and at grocers with well-stocked Asian food sections.

The Hostess-with-the-Mostest, Kathy Casey is known for her fancy yet not frivolous culinary creations. Your guests will sing the praises of this tasty cocktail nibble.

CHEF KATHY CASEY
ROSEMARY PARMESAN PUFFS

Kathy says, "Tiny cheesy gougères are delicious, and so retro-Frenchy. These habit-forming little morsels are perfect to pop as you sip a Mandarin Star cocktail."

Makes about 50 puffs

½ cup water

½ cup whole milk

6 tablespoons butter

1 tablespoon very finely minced fresh rosemary

½ teaspoon salt

1 tablespoon minced garlic

1 cup flour

4 large eggs

¾ cup grated high-quality Parmesan cheese

Place the water, milk, butter, rosemary, salt, and garlic in a heavy, medium-sized saucepan. Bring to a boil over medium-high heat.

All at once, add the flour and stir in quickly with a wooden spoon. Keep stirring—mixture will come away from the sides of the pan and become thick and stiff. Keep stirring and turning over for about 1 minute. (You want to dry the mixture out a bit.)

Transfer the mixture to a mixing bowl and, with a handheld or standing mixer, mix on medium-high speed. Add 1 egg. As soon as egg is partially incorporated, increase mixer speed to high. Add remaining eggs ONE AT A TIME when each previous egg is well incorporated. Mixture should be smooth. Mix in the Parmesan.

Preheat oven to 400°F. Line baking sheets with parchment paper. You will need 2 or 3 baking sheets, or work in batches. (If you don't have parchment, lightly spray baking sheets with nonstick vegetable spray and watch the cheese puff bottoms closely to prevent over-browning.) Drop mixture by heaping teaspoonfuls— they should be the size of large marbles—onto parchment; or you can pipe it from a large piping bag fitted with a large plain tip.

Bake on upper rack of oven for 22 to 25 minutes, or until puffs are golden. Serve warm.

If you're short of baking sheets, have more balls ready on sheets of parchment. When a batch of puffs is done, remove the baking sheet from the oven, pull off the parchment filled with cooked puffs, and quickly add the next parchment sheet of balls.

LIZ SMITH
WATERMELON TWIST

This drink is sure to be the talk of your next bash. A couple of these and you might even make the papers!

Makes 4 cocktails

3 cups seeded and cubed watermelon

Sea salt

Freshly ground black pepper

Vodka or gin

2 limes, halved

Liquefy the watermelon in a blender and strain through cheesecloth if it seems pulpy. Or process in a juicer.

Mix salt and pepper and place in a small saucer. Moisten rims of chilled martini glasses or other stemmed glasses, then dip in salt and pepper to frost the rims.

For each drink, fill a cocktail shaker glass with ice, then mix 3 ounces (6 tablespoons) watermelon juice with 1 shot of vodka or gin and the juice of half a lime. Shake vigorously, then strain into a chilled glass.

"The Grande Dame of the Dish," Liz Smith is an Emmy-winning reporter and syndicated columnist for the New York Daily News, Newsday, *and the* New York Post. *Your friends will want the inside scoop on this recipe!*

SOUPS & SALADS

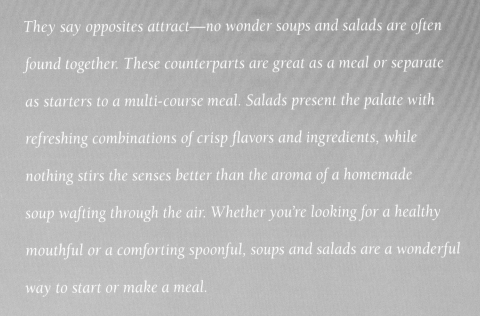

They say opposites attract—no wonder soups and salads are often found together. These counterparts are great as a meal or separate as starters to a multi-course meal. Salads present the palate with refreshing combinations of crisp flavors and ingredients, while nothing stirs the senses better than the aroma of a homemade soup wafting through the air. Whether you're looking for a healthy mouthful or a comforting spoonful, soups and salads are a wonderful way to start or make a meal.

Janet Hill's Gumbo—Grant Hill	34
Tropical Chicken Salad—Chris Evert	36
Mediterranean Vegetable Soup—Chef Graham Kerr	38
Water Island Scallop Corn Tomato Salad—Michael Kors	40
Salad of Black Mission Figs—Chef Thomas Keller	42
Benihana Salad Dressing—Chef Rocky H. Aoki	44
Ukrainian Borscht—Anna Kournikova	46
Fennel, Watermelon & Black Olive Salad—Chef Todd English	48
Shrimp Salad—Evelyn Lauder	50
Gami's Clam Chowder—Bill Gates	52
Chicken Noodle Soup—Rascal Flatts	53

JANET HILL'S GUMBO

Six-time NBA All-Star Grant Hill likes to make a roux from flour and butter to thicken the gumbo. He typically cooks a can of chicken broth in a skillet with a half cup of flour until it is browned, then adds that to the gumbo.

Makes 8 to 10 servings

½ chicken, about 1 ½ pounds, cut in pieces

6 cups water

1 ¼ to 1 ½ pounds okra

4 tablespoons (½ stick) butter

½ large onion, chopped (about 1 cup)

½ green bell pepper, chopped (about 1 cup)

1 ½ stalks celery, chopped (about ¾ cup)

1 bay leaf

¼ teaspoon dried basil

¼ teaspoon dried thyme

½ teaspoon salt

¼ teaspoon black pepper

1 garlic clove, minced

½ pound andouille sausage, cooked and sliced in bite-sized pieces

½ pound ham, cooked and cut in bite-sized cubes

1 teaspoon filé powder

½ teaspoon hot pepper sauce, or as needed

½ pound shrimp, washed, peeled and deveined, with tails on

½ pound crabmeat, picked through to remove any shells

"My gumbo is a Cajun not Creole variety. There are no tomatoes. I do use okra and filé, a spice that is indigenous to New Orleans. The gumbo is served hot over rice and eaten with a spoon. It is deceptively filling; two hours after eating it, you're hungry again!" Grant Hill

Place chicken pieces and water in a large pot and bring to a boil. Reduce heat and let simmer until done, about 1 hour. When done, remove chicken, saving water in pot for the base of the gumbo. Skim fat from broth if necessary. When chicken is cool enough to handle, remove and discard skin and bones, and cut chicken into bite-sized pieces. Reserve.

Meanwhile, wash the okra and cut off the ends. Dry okra between paper towels. Slice okra in rounds. Heat 3 tablespoons butter in a nonstick skillet and sauté the okra until all that's left is the okra. This takes 30 to 45 minutes. You must stir the okra throughout this process to keep it from sticking to the bottom of the pan. Reserve.

Add remaining butter to pan and sauté the onion, green pepper, and celery until lightly browned, about 8 to 10 minutes. Reserve.

When chicken broth is ready, stir in the cooked okra, sautéed vegetables, seasonings, garlic, and sausage, and bring to a simmer. Let simmer 15 to 20 minutes.

Stir in reserved chicken, ham, filé powder, and hot pepper sauce. (Important: Do not raise the heat above simmer after adding filé.) Add the shrimp and bring gumbo to a simmer to cook shrimp until just done, about 3 to 5 minutes.

Stir in crabmeat, and correct the seasoning with salt and pepper and hot sauce if desired. Serve in bowls over steaming hot rice.

Makes 4 servings

1 ¼ pounds boneless, skinless chicken breast, cooked and diced, or 4 cups diced cooked chicken

1 cup diced fresh pineapple

3 stalks celery, thinly sliced

½ cup thinly sliced green onions

¼ cup coarsely chopped dry-roasted unsalted peanuts

1 teaspoon salt

¼ teaspoon black pepper

3 tablespoons chutney, such as Major Grey's

2 tablespoons lemon juice

2 teaspoons grated or minced lemon zest

1 teaspoon curry powder

¾ cup mayonnaise or low-fat mayonnaise

Shredded or chopped romaine lettuce

Pineapple leaves for garnish, optional

CHRIS EVERT
TROPICAL CHICKEN SALAD

Tennis legend Chris Evert gives back to the game and to the community in every way she can, even in the kitchen. This delicious salad will definitely be to your advantage after a morning on the court. Chris likes to make it with low-fat, low-cholesterol mayonnaise.

Mix all ingredients together well. Serve as a light dinner or lunch on a bed of romaine. Garnish with pineapple leaves if desired.

Chris is one of the greatest tennis players of all time: she is the winner of 18 Grand Slam Championships and 157 tour single titles. She is pictured here with her family, from left to right, dog Lucky, husband Andy Mill, Nicky Mill, Chris Evert, Colton Mill, and Alex Mill.

Graham Kerr is a noted TV cooking personality and author. He is dedicated to helping people live healthy, nutritious, and creative lives. Graham is pictured here with his wife, Treena.

Makes 6 servings

1 teaspoon non-aromatic olive oil

½ pound sweet onions, chopped

2 garlic cloves, sliced

1 or 2 fennel bulbs, trimmed and cut in ½-inch cubes (about 1 cup)

¹⁄₁₆ teaspoon ground cloves

½ teaspoon finely chopped fresh rosemary, or ¼ teaspoon dried rosemary, crushed

1 (10 ¾-ounce) can tomato purée

2 European bay leaves

1 quart water

1 cup fresh fava beans or frozen baby lima beans

1 bunch spinach, washed, stemmed, and cut in strips

1 pound plum tomatoes, peeled, seeded, and chopped

¼ teaspoon black pepper

½ teaspoon salt

2 tablespoons chopped fennel tops or parsley, for garnish

CHEF GRAHAM KERR

MEDITERRANEAN VEGETABLE SOUP

"This Mediterranean spring soup celebrates the arrival of fava beans that flood farmers markets in season. Fresh favas have a nutty, sweet flavor and shouldn't be replaced with canned or dried, which are quite different." Graham Kerr

Heat the oil in a high-sided skillet on medium-high and sauté the onion until it begins to soften, about 3 minutes. Stir in the garlic and cook 1 minute more. Add the fennel, cloves, rosemary, tomato purée, bay leaves, and water. Bring to a boil, drop in the beans, and simmer 5 minutes, or until beans are tender.

Add the spinach, tomatoes, pepper, and salt. Simmer 4 more minutes. Remove the bay leaves and serve topped with the chopped fennel or parsley.

MICHAEL KORS
WATER ISLAND SCALLOP CORN TOMATO SALAD

Quintessentially summer, this fashionable salad shows the season's collection at its best. Michael recommends serving it with chilled Greco di Tufo Italian white wine and toasted ciabatta bread.

Fashion designer Michael Kors actually sent his only copy of this photo of him and his mom, Joan Kors. Thank you for sharing one of your most cherished possessions with us.

Makes 6 to 8 servings

2 tablespoons olive oil

4 ears corn, shucked and kernels cut from cobs (about 2½ cups kernels)

¼ cup dry white wine

1 pound sea scallops, quartered

4 large, ripe beefsteak tomatoes, diced (about 4 cups)

½ cup fresh basil leaves, coarsely chopped

½ cup extra-virgin olive oil

Juice of 2 lemons (⅓ cup juice)

2 teaspoons minced garlic

¼ teaspoon freshly ground white pepper

Lots of freshly ground sea salt (about 1 to 2 teaspoons)

In a sauté pan, heat 2 tablespoons olive oil until hot. Sauté corn about 3 minutes, or until just tender. Remove corn to a large bowl. In the same sauté pan, add wine and bring to a simmer. Add the scallops, cover, and simmer until just cooked, about 2 to 3 minutes. With a slotted spoon, remove scallops to a strainer to drain.

To the corn, add the drained scallops and remaining ingredients. Let marinate, covered, for at least 30 minutes before serving so that flavors can mingle.

Thomas Keller is the internationally renowned owner and chef of the French Laundry restaurant in Napa Valley, as well as restaurants in Las Vegas and New York.

Makes 6 servings

6 large or 9 medium fresh figs, preferably Black Mission

Extra-virgin olive oil

Balsamic vinegar

¼ cup very finely minced shallots

Kosher salt

1 red bell pepper, roasted, peeled, and cut into ¼-inch julienne (see method below)

1 yellow bell pepper, roasted, peeled, and cut into ¼-inch julienne

1 small fennel bulb, top trimmed down to the bulb

¼ cup Fennel Oil (recipe follows)

1 tablespoon Balsamic Glaze (recipe follows)

2 tablespoons fennel seeds, toasted and finely ground

CHEF THOMAS KELLER

SALAD OF BLACK MISSION FIGS

WITH ROASTED SWEET PEPPERS AND SHAVED FENNEL

"I love the licorice flavor in plants such as fennel and tarragon. This salad is really about the Napa Valley, where we have the same problem of overabundance of figs as most people do with tomatoes." Thomas Keller

Slice the figs into rounds about ¼ inch thick. You will need a total of 18 slices. Place them on a plate, and drizzle lightly with olive oil and balsamic vinegar. Sprinkle with 2 tablespoons shallots and salt to taste. Let them marinate for 1 hour at room temperature.

Meanwhile, toss the roasted peppers with the remaining shallots and olive oil, balsamic vinegar, and salt to taste. Let marinate for 1 hour.

Holding the fennel bulb by the stem end, cut it on a mandoline into paper-thin slices. You will need at least ½ cup. Place the shaved fennel in a bowl of cold water to crisp; it can be held for a few hours this way.

To complete the salad: Stir the fennel oil and balsamic glaze together. They will not emulsify, and the balsamic glaze should bead in the oil. Set aside.

Drain the shaved fennel and dry on a towel. Toss the fennel with a bit of olive oil, balsamic vinegar, and salt to taste. Center a round of fig on each serving plate. Twirl a few strips of the julienned peppers around a fork, place the peppers on a fig slice, and top with another slice of fig. Repeat the process so that there are 3 slices of figs and 2 layers of peppers, then repeat with the remaining plates. Stack the fennel salad on top of the fig slices. Drizzle the fennel oil/balsamic glaze mixture around the plates and sprinkle the plates with the ground fennel seed.

Roasted Peppers

Preheat oven to 350°F. Line a baking sheet with foil. Cut the peppers in half lengthwise. Trim and discard the white ribs and seeds. Brush the peppers with olive oil and place cut side down on the baking sheet. Bake for 15 to 20 minutes, or until they have softened and the skin has loosened from the flesh. Place in a covered container for several minutes to steam and loosen the skin further. When cool enough to handle, peel off skin and discard any remaining seeds or ribs.

Fennel Oil

Makes about ⅓ cup

2 cups fennel fronds

2 cups Italian parsley sprigs

About ¾ cup canola oil

Bring a large pot of salted water to a boil. (Use about ¼ cup kosher salt per quart of water.) Place herbs in a strainer and dip them into the water for 10 to 15 seconds, keeping the water at a strong boil. Remove the strainer and immediately plunge the blanched herbs into an ice-water bath to chill.

Drain herbs and squeeze as dry as possible. Use scissors to cut them into small pieces.

Place half the herbs in a blender with enough of the oil to just cover. Blend herbs on medium speed for 1 minute. If herbs aren't turning freely, add slightly more oil. Turn the speed to high and blend for another 2 minutes. Check the oil occasionally. It will become slightly warm, but it should not get too hot or there will be some loss of color. If purée warms up too much, refrigerate to cool.

Add half of the remaining herbs to the blender and blend for another 2 minutes. Then add remaining herbs and blend for 2 more minutes. Remove the purée to a container and refrigerate for at least a day; can be stored for up to 1 week. Once strained, the oil will normally discolor in 2 days. It can be frozen for several weeks, however.

Place a piece of cheesecloth over a container and secure with a rubber band or string. Place the purée on the cheesecloth and let the oil filter through for about an hour. Discard the cheesecloth and remaining purée—don't wring out the cheesecloth or you may cloud the oil. Store in fridge or freeze. Put in a small plastic squeeze bottle for garnishing dishes.

Balsamic Glaze

Makes ½ cup

2 cups balsamic vinegar

Heat vinegar in a heavy saucepan over medium heat until steam rises from the liquid. Place the saucepan on a heat diffuser and let the liquid reduce very slowly (it shouldn't simmer) for 2 to 3 hours, or until it has reduced and thickened to a syrupy glaze.

Rocky Aoki, pictured here with his wife, Keiko, is the founder and owner of Benihana. With brains and brawn (he is also a former Olympic wrestler), Rocky knows how to cook up a good time.

Makes about ¾ cup, enough dressing for 6 starter salads

¼ cup chopped onion

¼ cup peanut oil or other vegetable oil

2 tablespoons unseasoned rice wine vinegar

2 tablespoons water

1 tablespoon chopped fresh ginger

1 tablespoon chopped celery

1 tablespoon soy sauce

1 ½ teaspoons tomato paste

1 ½ teaspoons sugar

1 teaspoon lemon juice

¼ teaspoon salt

⅛ teaspoon black pepper

CHEF ROCKY H. AOKI
BENIHANA SALAD DRESSING

The famed Benihana Restaurants really were the first to introduce the interactive kitchen to America. This signature dressing is excellent tossed with a mixture of your favorite greens—especially one that includes peppery mizuna fancifully garnished with vegetable curls of carrot, beet and daikon radish.

Combine all ingredients in a blender container or work bowl of a food processor fitted with a steel knife.

Process until almost smooth.

This can be kept refrigerated for up to 1 week.

Tennis star, model, and actor, Anna Kournikova excels on the court, in the studio, and even in the kitchen!

ANNA KOURNIKOVA
UKRAINIAN BORSCHT

Anna's pretty-in-pink soup serves a powerful flavor punch—only Anna can make borscht look this sexy.

To make the stock: Place the beef, marrowbones, spareribs, and stock vegetables in a 4- to 5-quart pot. Add water and salt, and bring to a boil. Lower the heat and simmer, partially covered, for about 1 1/2 hours, or until the beef is tender.

Remove the meat, cover and reserve. Strain the stock, discarding the vegetables, and skim off the fat. Add salt to taste.

To finish and serve the soup: In a heavy skillet, heat the butter over medium to medium-high heat and sauté the onion, potato, carrot, celery root, cabbage, and garlic for 4 minutes, stirring often. Add beets and tomatoes, and sauté 2 minutes more, stirring often.

Bring the stock to a boil, add the sautéed vegetables, black pepper, and tomato paste, and simmer for 8 minutes more. Remove from the heat. While the vegetables are cooking, strip the pork off the bones and cut the meat into bite-sized pieces. Discard bones. Add all the meat, parsley, and dill to the soup. Thin soup with a little hot water if needed. Cover and let stand for 10 minutes before serving.

Pass a bowl of sour cream.

Makes 8 servings

Stock

1 pound boneless beef chuck
or stew meat, cut in 1/2-inch chunks

1/2 pound beef marrowbones

1/2 pound pork spareribs

1 onion, chopped

1/2 carrot, chopped

1/2 cup chopped celery root

3 quarts water

1 teaspoon salt

1 tablespoon butter

1 onion, sliced lengthwise into strips
(about 2 cups)

1 large russet potato, peeled and cut in
1/2-inch dice (about 2 cups)

1 carrot, cut into thin matchstick strips
(about 1 cup)

3/4 cup thin matchstick strips celery root

1/3 head cabbage, cored and cut into
1-inch squares (about 4 cups)

2 garlic cloves, crushed or finely chopped

3 beets, peeled and shredded
(about 2 1/2 to 3 cups)

3 tomatoes, chopped (about 2 cups)

1/2 teaspoon freshly ground black pepper

2 tablespoons tomato paste

1 tablespoon finely chopped parsley

1 tablespoon finely chopped fresh dill

Sour cream, for garnish

Makes 6 to 8 servings

1 to 2 fennel bulbs, thinly sliced on a Japanese mandoline (about 2 cups)

4 cups seeded watermelon chunks

½ cup coarsely chopped black olives

1 red onion, thinly sliced (about 2 cups)

1 bunch green onions, green part only, chopped

¼ cup chopped fresh basil leaves

1 ½ to 2 cups crumbled Bulgarian feta cheese

¼ cup fresh lemon juice

½ cup extra-virgin olive oil

2 tablespoons balsamic vinegar

1 teaspoon kosher salt

½ teaspoon black pepper

CHEF TODD ENGLISH

FENNEL, WATERMELON & BLACK OLIVE SALAD
WITH FETA CHEESE

Place the fennel, watermelon, black olives, red onion, green onion, basil, and feta in a large bowl. Add the lemon juice, oil, vinegar, salt, and pepper and toss well. Divide among salad plates and serve immediately.

Chef and restaurateur Todd English, named by People *magazine as one of 2001's 50 most beautiful people, presents a dish with exciting and bold flavor combinations.*

Makes 4 servings

1 ½ pounds cooked bay shrimp, drained well

1 small Savoy cabbage or Chinese cabbage, thinly sliced

2 green onions, thinly sliced

2 stalks celery, thinly sliced on the bias

¼ cup coarsely chopped cilantro

½ cup sliced water chestnuts

¼ cup chopped salted peanuts, optional

Topping

½ cup thin matchstick strips carrot

Crispy rice noodles*

Dressing

2 tablespoons toasted sesame oil

⅓ cup rice wine vinegar

2 tablespoons water

1 tablespoon sugar

1 teaspoon toasted sesame seeds

2 tablespoons thick teriyaki sauce

Evelyn Lauder is senior corporate vice president of The Estee Lauder Companies and founder and chairman of The Breast Cancer Research Foundation.

EVELYN LAUDER
SHRIMP SALAD

Evelyn also likes making this fresh and bright salad with chicken instead of shrimp; either way, it's perfect as a starter salad or light supper entrée.

Combine shrimp with remaining salad ingredients. Separately, toss topping ingredients together.

To make the dressing: Stir all ingredients together. Reserve.

Just before serving, toss the salad with the dressing. Serve salad sprinkled with topping.

*Crispy rice noodles are made by frying saifun noodles. You can also substitute any other crisp fried Asian noodle.

Makes 6 to 8 servings

1 pound bacon, chopped

2 tablespoons butter

1 ½ cups finely chopped onions*

2 cups finely chopped carrots*

2 cups diced russet potatoes

½ cup water

1 quart half-and-half

5 (6.5-ounce) cans minced or chopped clams

2 tablespoons butter, optional

2 tablespoons flour, optional

Salt and black pepper

Microsoft Chairman William (Bill) H. Gates, pictured here with his sister Libby Gates Armintrout, began programming computers as a young teen. His vision of personal technology revolutionized computer use. As philanthropists, the Gates family has made major commitments in education and health.

BILL GATES
GAMI'S CLAM CHOWDER

A Gates family favorite and a Northwest comfort food, this chowder should be very thick with tender vegetables.

In a large Dutch oven or soup kettle over medium heat, fry the bacon until crisp. With a slotted spoon, remove bacon to paper towels to drain.

Reserve one-quarter of the bacon fat in the pan, discarding remainder. Add 2 tablespoons butter and sauté the onions until golden brown. Then add the carrots, potatoes, and water, increase the heat to high, and immediately cover the pan. Steam until vegetables are just tender, about 10 minutes.

Add half-and-half, bacon, and clams in juice. Bring to a low boil and then reduce heat to a simmer.

To make the mixture slightly thicker, if desired, melt 2 tablespoons butter in a small saucepan and stir in 2 tablespoons flour. Whisk the butter-flour mixture into the hot chowder and cook about 5 minutes, or until slightly thickened. Season with salt and pepper to taste.

*Vegetables must be finely chopped. The Gateses use a heavy-duty blender, but a food processor will work as well.

Makes 4 to 6 entrée servings

1 small onion, chopped (about ½ cup)

2 stalks celery, sliced (about 1 cup)

2 carrots, sliced (about 1 cup)

2 garlic cloves, finely chopped

1 teaspoon dried parsley flakes

1 teaspoon dried thyme leaves

1 (14.5-ounce) can diced tomatoes in juice

4 (14-ounce) cans reduced-sodium chicken broth

1 bay leaf

1 cup of your favorite dry soup noodle, such as orzo, stelle, acini di pepe, alphabets, etc.

¾ pound cooked chicken, diced (about 2 cups)

1 cup frozen peas

Salt and black pepper

The 2003 ACM and CMA Vocal Group of the Year, Rascal Flatts enjoy slurping this soup down in between hit singles; with albums going double platinum, these guys need their energy. And you'll be loving this soup out loud too for its simplicity and down-home flavors.

RASCAL FLATTS
CHICKEN NOODLE SOUP

Spray a heavy soup pot with nonstick vegetable spray. Heat pot over medium heat and sauté the onion, celery, and carrots until fragrant and starting to brown, about 5 to 6 minutes. Stir in the garlic, parsley, and thyme, and sauté 30 seconds more. Do not brown the garlic.

Add the tomatoes and stir well, dissolving any browned bits on bottom of pot. Add the broth and bay leaf, and bring to a boil.

Stir in the pasta, and continue to stir until soup returns to a boil. Cook pasta until al dente, about 6 to 10 minutes, or according to package directions.

Stir in the chicken and peas, and season with salt and pepper to taste. Return soup to a simmer and cook until chicken is just heated through.

MAIN COURSES

Main dishes are the star of the show for any meal and the center of the plate. From steak to salmon to chicken, the main course is a great way to utilize local and regional products or to experiment with ingredients from beyond your backyard. Treat your main course like a star and your guests will rave with satisfaction. Don't be afraid to take a chance and try something new: who knows, your favorite celebrity's most treasured recipe could become yours, too.

Uptown Marinated Skirt Steak—Billy Joel   56

Chicken Piccata with Pine Nuts & Capers—Florence Henderson   58

Salmon Burgers—Candice Bergen   60

Seared Wild Salmon with Summer Fruit Salsa—Tom Skerritt   62

Bronzed Steak with Gingersnap Gravy—Chef Paul Prudhomme   64

Veal Shanks Braised with Rum
    over Coconut Mashed Sweet Potatoes—Chef Emeril Lagasse   65

Lemon Chicken—Katie Couric   66

Filet de Boeuf Béarnaise—Andy Roddick   68

Seared Lamb Chops with Rosemary and Mint Sauce—Chef Lidia Bastianich   70

Grilled Rib Steaks with Panzanella—Chef Tom Douglas   71

Pompano with Citrus Crust and Grapefruit Butter Sauce—Chef Emeril Lagasse   72

Herb Roast Turkey—Andre Agassi & Stefanie Graf   74

Swordfish Provençal—Chef Sheila Lukins   76

Chicken Sauterne—Paul G. Allen   78

Jambalaya—Harry Connick, Jr.   79

Singer/songwriter and Piano Man Billy Joel is a musical legend. Not only are his tunes tasty, but his skirt steak also rocks.

BILLY JOEL

UPTOWN MARINATED SKIRT STEAK

Billy sent in this recipe made with skirt steak, which is a delicious and full-flavored cut of meat but can sometimes be hard to find. It works just as well with flank steak, which is best cooked rare to medium-rare and sliced thin. Serve with fresh lime squeezed over the top if desired.

Mix oils, garlic, lime juice, and teriyaki sauce in a heavy zip-top plastic bag. Add steak to marinade. Move steak around in bag to coat. Close the bag, pressing out air. Let steak marinate in the refrigerator for at least 2 hours or up to 24 hours.

Heat grill until very hot. Remove steak from marinade and season with salt and pepper to taste. Grill on each side for about 2 to 4 minutes, or until cooked to desired doneness. Remove from the grill and slice thin.

Makes 4 servings

¼ cup olive oil

1 tablespoon Asian sesame oil

2 tablespoons minced garlic

¼ cup fresh lime juice

¼ cup teriyaki sauce

1 flank or skirt steak, about 1 ¾ pounds

Salt and freshly ground black pepper

FLORENCE HENDERSON

CHICKEN PICCATA
WITH PINE NUTS AND CAPERS

Makes 4 servings

¼ cup milk

2 large eggs, slightly beaten

½ cup flour

1 ½ teaspoons salt

¼ teaspoon black pepper

4 (6-ounce) boneless, skinless chicken breast halves, pounded to ½-inch thickness

4 tablespoons (½ stick) butter

2 tablespoons vegetable oil

⅓ cup lemon juice

⅓ cup white wine, or substitute apple juice, white grape juice, or chicken broth

2 garlic cloves, chopped

2 tablespoons capers, drained

¼ cup minced fresh parsley

½ pound dry pasta, cooked al dente, then tossed with ¼ cup olive oil

¼ cup toasted pine nuts

To flatten the chicken breasts, place between two pieces of plastic wrap. With a meat mallet or rolling pin, lightly and evenly pound the chicken to the desired thickness, taking care not to tear holes in the meat.

In a small, flat bowl, mix together the milk and eggs. In another flat dish, mix the flour, salt, and pepper.

Dip the chicken pieces into the milk mixture and then into the flour mixture. Coat each piece well, then shake off the excess.

Meanwhile, in a large, shallow nonstick skillet over medium-high heat, heat 2 tablespoons of the butter and all the vegetable oil. Add the coated chicken pieces to the hot skillet and cook until the chicken is no longer pink on the inside, about 2 to 3 minutes on each side. Drain chicken on paper towels. Keep warm.

Reduce the heat to medium-low and add the remaining 2 tablespoons of butter to the pan drippings. Stir in the lemon juice, wine, and garlic. Cook for 2 to 3 minutes, stirring well.

Add the capers and half the parsley. Cook, stirring, for about 1 minute.

To serve, toss pasta with remaining parsley and place a serving of pasta on each plate. Top with a chicken breast. Spoon some sauce over each and sprinkle with pine nuts. Serve immediately.

Makes 4 servings

1 ½ pounds boneless, skinless salmon fillet

¼ cup chopped shallots

2 teaspoons chopped fresh dill

1 tablespoon fresh lemon juice

2 tablespoons nonfat cottage cheese

2 egg yolks

¾ teaspoon salt

¼ teaspoon black pepper

Olive oil

Yogurt Dill Sauce
Makes ¾ cup

½ cup nonfat yogurt

1 tablespoon lemon juice

2 teaspoons minced garlic

½ teaspoon salt

¼ teaspoon black pepper

1 tablespoon chopped fresh dill

¼ cup grated, and squeezed dry,
English cucumber

"Evelyn Lauder gave me a list of her friends to ask to participate in this book. One of these friends was actor Candice Bergen. Unbeknownst to me, I was given Candice's home phone number. When she personally answered the phone, I felt like a phone solicitor. Even though she was in the middle of something very important, she was very gracious. Thank you, Candice, for your support, and I promise not to pass your number around."
Tami Agassi

CANDICE BERGEN
SALMON BURGERS

These light and healthy salmon cakes are scrumptious served on a bed of crisp greens or stacked on toasted buns as a burger alternative. Yogurt Dill Sauce was added to Candice's recipe as the perfect tangy accompaniment.

Finely chop the salmon, or cut into chunks, then pulse in food processor until finely chopped (do not purée).

Combine salmon with remaining ingredients except oil. Mix well, then shape into 4 patties, ½ to ¾ inch thick.

Brush a nonstick frying pan with olive oil. Fry the salmon cakes over medium-high heat, turning so that they are crisp and golden on the outside but medium-rare on the inside, about 2 ½ to 3 minutes per side.

Serve with Yogurt Dill Sauce.

To make the Yogurt Dill Sauce, mix the yogurt, lemon juice, garlic, salt, and pepper. Stir in dill and cucumber.

Refrigerate, covered, until ready to serve.

Makes 4 servings

Salsa

2 cups pitted, halved fresh Bing cherries, or diced apricots, nectarines, peaches, or pears

2 tablespoons seasoned rice wine vinegar

¼ cup minced Walla Walla Sweet onion, or other sweet onion

1 tablespoon chopped fresh cilantro

1 ½ teaspoons very finely minced fresh ginger

¼ to ½ teaspoon, depending on how spicy you like it, red pepper flakes or sambal oelek Asian chili paste

Salmon

4 (6- to 8-ounce) pieces thick, boneless, skinless wild salmon fillet

Salt and black pepper

2 tablespoons olive oil

TOM SKERRITT

SEARED WILD SALMON
WITH SUMMER FRUIT SALSA

Scrumptious wild salmon gets topped with zingy fruit salsa in this sublime Seattle-style dish. Washington red wines such as Merlot or Syrah are delicious paired with salmon.

In a small bowl, gently mix together all salsa ingredients. This is best if made right before serving but can be made up to 2 hours in advance.

Preheat oven to 450°F.

Season salmon on each side with salt and pepper. Heat the oil over medium heat in a large ovenproof skillet until hot. Place salmon, top side down, in skillet and sear until lightly golden. Turn salmon over and sear about a minute more.

Place pan of salmon in preheated oven until just done and slightly opaque in the center. (The timing will vary depending on the thickness of your salmon, so check it often. It shouldn't take more than a couple of minutes.)

Place each piece of salmon on a warm plate and top with ¼ cup of the salsa. Serve remaining salsa on the side.

*Pictured here with his wife, Julie Tokashiki, and their cat, Zoey, actor and director
Tom Skerritt is definitely a Top Gun. Like this recipe, he and Julie are truly Northwest.*

Paul Prudhomme is one of America's best-known chefs. Owner of the renowned restaurant K-Paul's Louisiana Kitchen and Magic Seasoning Blends in New Orleans, Chef Paul is also a best-selling author.

CHEF PAUL PRUDHOMME
BRONZED STEAK
WITH GINGERSNAP GRAVY

Makes 4 to 6 servings

Seasoning Mix

3 tablespoons Chef Paul Prudhomme's Meat Magic®

1 ¾ teaspoons ground ginger

1 teaspoon dry mustard

3 tablespoons unsalted butter

1 cup chopped onions

½ cup chopped red bell pepper

½ cup chopped yellow bell pepper

1 teaspoon minced garlic

2 teaspoons minced fresh ginger

About 2 cups chicken stock, preferred, or vegetable stock, in all (see note)

⅓ cup gingersnap cookies, broken in pieces

1 cup heavy cream

2 tablespoons vegetable oil or olive oil

4 to 6 beef tenderloin steaks, about ½ inch thick, or other favorite steak

When he sent in this recipe, Paul noted, "Each time we tested this recipe, we used a different brand of gingersnaps, and they all had different tastes and thickening properties, so you may need to add a little more or less stock to the sauce to obtain the thickness you want." If making the recipe for 4 people, keep the extra sauce for another day.

Combine the seasoning mix ingredients in a small bowl.

Heat the butter in a 10-inch skillet over medium-high heat. As soon as it melts, stir in 1 ½ tablespoons of the seasoning mix. When the butter is sizzling and foamy, add the onions and all the bell peppers. Stir well, then cover and cook for 6 minutes. Uncover, stir, and scrape up any brown bits sticking to the bottom of the skillet. The vegetables will be brightly colored and just beginning to brown. Re-cover and continue to cook for 6 more minutes, stirring and scraping occasionally.

Stir in the garlic, ginger, and 1 teaspoon of the seasoning mix. Stir well, then add 1 cup of the stock and stir and scrape until all the browned material is dissolved. The mixture should be a red-brown color. Re-cover and cook for 8 minutes, then whisk in the gingersnaps and the remaining 1 cup of stock. Cook, uncovered, whisking frequently, until the mixture is smooth, about 3 minutes. Gradually whisk in the cream, bring to a boil, then reduce the heat to medium and simmer, whisking frequently, until the gravy has thickened to the consistency of heavy cream, about 10 minutes. Makes about 3 cups.

Spread ½ teaspoon of oil on each side of the steaks. Season steaks evenly with ½ teaspoon of the seasoning mix per side.

Place a 12-inch nonstick skillet over high heat just until the pan is hot. Place the steaks in the pan and cook, turning once, until they are just cooked through (medium), about 3 to 4 minutes per side. The steaks are properly cooked when somewhat firm to the touch. Serve immediately, with one steak and ½ cup of sauce per serving.

CHEF EMERIL LAGASSE
VEAL SHANKS
BRAISED WITH RUM OVER COCONUT MASHED SWEET POTATOES

Emeril likes to accompany this dish with black beans seasoned with garlic and thyme.

Preheat oven to 325°F.

Season the shanks generously with salt and pepper. Dredge the shanks in the flour and pat off excess.

Heat a 6-quart Dutch oven over medium-high heat until hot. Add and heat the olive oil, then brown the shanks on all sides, about 4 minutes per side. Remove from the pot and reserve on a plate.

Add the onion, carrot, and celery, and sauté for 3 minutes, scraping the pan often to prevent sticking. Reduce the heat, add the tomato paste, and cook for an additional 2 minutes. Return the shanks to the pot and add ¼ cup of the rum, cinnamon sticks, bay leaves, thyme, broth, and brown sugar. Bring to a simmer and add the jalapeño pepper. Cover and place in preheated oven to simmer gently for about 2 hours, or until meat is tender and falling off the bone.

Gently remove the veal shanks from the pot and keep warm. Remove the bay leaves, cinnamon sticks, and jalapeño pepper from the sauce. Working in small batches, purée the sauce in a blender. Return sauce to pot and reduce on high until thickened and saucy. You should have about 2 cups of sauce. Taste and season with cayenne, Worcestershire sauce, hot sauce, lime juice, an additional splash of rum, and salt and pepper if needed.

Pour the thickened sauce back over the shanks and serve warm with the Coconut Mashed Sweet Potatoes.

Coconut Mashed Sweet Potatoes

Preheat oven to 350°F.

Rub sweet potatoes with olive oil, place on a baking sheet, and bake until they are completely tender, about 45 minutes to 1¼ hours.

Let the sweet potatoes cool for 5 minutes, or until just cool enough to handle. Split the potatoes lengthwise with a sharp knife and use a spoon to scrape out the insides into a medium bowl. Add the remaining ingredients and mash with a fork. Adjust seasoning with salt and pepper.

Makes 4 servings

4 12- to 16-ounce milk-fed veal shanks
Salt and black pepper
¼ cup flour
2 tablespoons olive oil
1 onion, diced
2 carrots, diced
2 stalks celery, diced
1 tablespoon tomato paste
¼ cup spiced dark rum, plus a splash more
2 cinnamon sticks
2 bay leaves
1 teaspoon fresh thyme
2 cups low-sodium beef broth
1 tablespoon brown sugar
1 pickled jalapeño pepper
Cayenne pepper
Worcestershire sauce
Hot pepper sauce
Freshly squeezed lime juice

Coconut Mashed Sweet Potatoes
Makes 6 to 8 servings

3 medium sweet potatoes
1 teaspoon olive oil
½ cup unsweetened coconut milk
¼ cup sour cream
2 tablespoons Steen's cane syrup
1 teaspoon ground cinnamon
⅛ teaspoon grated nutmeg
¼ teaspoon salt
1/16 teaspoon ground white pepper

Makes 4 servings

4 boneless, skinless chicken breast halves (about 1 ¼ to 1 ½ pounds total)

Salt and black pepper

Flour for dredging

2 tablespoons butter

2 tablespoons olive oil

3 tablespoons flour

Juice of 2 lemons

3 cups chicken stock or low-sodium canned chicken broth

Ground white pepper

2 tablespoons chopped parsley, for garnish

Lemon slices, for garnish

Katie Couric is co-anchor of Today, *contributing anchor for* Dateline NBC, *and co-founder of the National Colorectal Cancer Research Alliance (NCCRA). "Katie Couric is a perfect example of the six degrees of separation. My college roommate happens to be friends with Katie's neighbor. Thank you, Katie, for saying yes." Tami Agassi*

KATIE COURIC
LEMON CHICKEN

If you love lemon, this is your recipe! Katie likes to serve the chicken on a bed of basmati rice.

Pound chicken breasts with a meat mallet to a uniform ⅓-inch thickness. Season chicken on both sides with salt and pepper to taste. Place flour on a large plate and dredge chicken lightly in the flour, shaking off excess.

Meanwhile, in a large sauté pan over medium-high heat, melt the butter and oil until it sizzles. Add the chicken breasts and sauté, turning once or twice, until almost cooked through and chicken is golden on both sides, about 3 to 4 minutes per side. Remove chicken and set aside.

Whisk the 3 tablespoons flour into drippings in pan and cook, stirring, for 1 minute. Whisk in lemon juice and chicken stock. Bring to a boil, then reduce heat to a simmer. Return chicken to pan to finish cooking until juices run clear, and let sauce reduce until thickened. Season to taste with salt and white pepper.

Spoon the sauce over the chicken to serve. Garnish with chopped parsley and lemon slices.

ANDY RODDICK
FILET DE BOEUF BÉARNAISE

This is one of Andy's favorite dishes from Chef Philippe Lajaunie, owner of Les Halles Restaurant in New York. "This can be a tough sauce. But keep trying. It's worth it. Once you get it down, you can pretty much rule the world." Philippe Lajaunie

Makes 4 servings

4 beef tenderloin steaks, about 8 ounces each

Freshly ground black pepper

1 teaspoon oil

Sea salt

Tarragon sprigs

Béarnaise Sauce

½ cup white wine vinegar

2 tablespoons finely chopped shallots

1 teaspoon cracked black peppercorns

1 small bunch fresh tarragon, finely chopped (include some stems)

16 tablespoons (2 sticks) butter

4 egg yolks

Salt and black pepper

Remove the meat from refrigeration about 10 minutes before cooking. Season with pepper on all sides, then brush with oil.

If grilling outdoors, preheat the grill to high. Once the grill is hot, place the beef on the surface. Cook for 1 minute, then rotate beef 90 degrees to create that slick-looking checkerboard pattern you see in restaurants and advertisements. After another minute, turn the steaks over and repeat the process. Move the steaks to a less hot area of the grill and continue cooking—2 to 4 minutes for rare, 6 to 8 minutes for medium-rare.

If cooking indoors, place a cast-iron grill pan over high heat, using two burners if the size of the pan allows. Place the seasoned, oiled meat in the pan. After 2 minutes, rotate the meat 90 degrees. After another 2 minutes, turn the meat over and repeat the process. Cook to desired doneness.

Salt the steaks to taste. Serve steaks generously dolloped with Béarnaise sauce and garnished with sprigs of fresh tarragon. Pass extra sauce.

To make the sauce: In a saucepan, combine the vinegar, shallots, cracked pepper, and tarragon. Bring to a boil and reduce until it has a pastelike consistency and almost all liquid has evaporated. Remove from heat and set aside.

Meanwhile, place butter in a saucepan over low heat. As the butter melts, foam will rise to the top. Skim the foam and discard. Remove melted butter from the heat and set aside so that the milk solids settle to the bottom.

Place the egg yolks in a stainless steel mixing bowl. Whisk in the tarragon reduction. Bring some water to a simmer in the bottom of a double-boiler, and place the metal bowl with the yolks and reduction over the water, whisking constantly. Do not let the bottom of the bowl touch the water, and do not let the water boil. Pull the whole bowl away from the heat if the eggs start to look like they might scramble; continue to whisk as the eggs start to become foamy.

Once the eggs become aerated and slightly foamy and thick, slowly begin drizzling in the clarified butter, whisking as you go to form an emulsion. (Use only the clarified butter, not the milk solids.) When all the butter is neatly incorporated into a lovely, fully emulsified sauce, season with salt and pepper to taste. Adjust the consistency of the sauce with a tiny bit of warm water if necessary.

Serve immediately or, if you need to hold the sauce for more than 10 minutes, place in a small thermos.

Chef Lidia Bastianich is co-owner with her son, Joseph, of Felidia and Becco restaurants in New York and Lidia's in Kansas City and Pittsburgh. She is also a cookbook author and star of Lidia's Italian-American Kitchen *and* Lidia's Italian Table.

Makes 4 servings

Lamb

12 "frenched" rib lamb chops, about 3 pounds total (see Note)

1 tablespoon fresh rosemary leaves

2 teaspoons extra-virgin olive oil

1 teaspoon salt

1 teaspoon freshly ground black pepper

Mint sprigs, for garnish

Sauce

1 orange

1 pound meaty lamb bones, or lamb shank cut in 3 to 4 pieces by butcher

3 tablespoons extra-virgin olive oil

1 tablespoon flour

½ cup chopped onions

¼ cup sliced carrots

¼ cup sliced celery

1 tablespoon chopped fresh sage leaves

1 tablespoon chopped fresh rosemary leaves

1 tablespoon chopped fresh mint leaves

3 cups homemade chicken stock or canned low-sodium chicken broth

½ cup dry white wine

Salt and freshly ground black pepper

CHEF LIDIA BASTIANICH

SEARED LAMB CHOPS
WITH ROSEMARY AND MINT SAUCE

This recipe takes a while to prepare and you'll need to plan ahead a bit, but when you taste this sauce, you'll be proud of every minute you invested.

Rub the chops with the rosemary, oil, salt, and pepper, and let them stand at room temperature for up to 2 hours or refrigerate, covered, for up to 1 day.

Start the sauce the day before serving. Preheat oven to 425°F. With a vegetable peeler, remove zest from orange, juice the orange, and reserve zest and juice separately.

Trim the lamb scraps from the chops of all fat, and combine scraps with the lamb bones in a roasting pan. (If using lamb shank, cut away the meat to expose bone and place bones and trim in pan.) Pour 1 tablespoon of the olive oil over the trimmings and bones, and toss to coat. Roast for 30 minutes. Sprinkle the flour over the bones and roast until the bones are well browned, about another 15 minutes.

Meanwhile, in a large nonreactive saucepan, heat the remaining oil over medium heat. Add the onions and cook, stirring occasionally, until softened, about 5 minutes. Add the carrots, celery, sage, rosemary, mint, and orange zest. Cook, stirring occasionally, until the vegetables are lightly browned, about 5 minutes. If the vegetables begin to stick, add a small amount of the chicken stock and stir well.

Transfer the browned bones and meat scraps to the saucepan. Pour off and discard all the fat from the roasting pan. While the roasting pan is still hot, add the wine and orange juice, and scrape up and dissolve the browned bits. Add the remaining chicken stock and continue to scrape the bottom of the pan to release all the browned drippings. Scrape everything from the roasting pan into the saucepan and bring to a boil over high heat. Reduce the heat to a simmer and cook, frequently skimming the foam and fat from the surface, until the liquid is reduced to approximately 1 ½ cups, about 1 ¼ hours.

Discard the bones and strain the sauce through a fine sieve, pressing down hard on the solids to squeeze as much liquid as possible from them. Refrigerate the sauce overnight to let fat come to the top and solidify.

Remove excess fat. Return the sauce to a saucepan and simmer over low heat until reduced to the consistency of gravy, about ½ cup. Adjust the seasoning with salt and pepper if desired. Cover and keep warm.

Heat a heavy griddle or large cast-iron skillet over medium-high heat. Add as many chops as will fit without touching and cook, turning once, until well browned outside and rosy pink in the center, about 2 minutes per side. (For more well-done chops, add 1 to 2 minutes to the cooking time.) Repeat with any remaining chops.

Spoon the sauce onto plates and arrange the chops over the sauce, with the bones crossing. Decorate with mint sprigs.

Note: Ask the butcher to french the chops, or do it yourself: Cut the meat and fat away from each rib bone, starting at the point where the "eye" of meat meets the bone. Scrape the bone clean with the back side of a knife. There should be from 1 ½ to 3 inches of bone protruding. Save all trimmings from the chops to use in the sauce.

70

Chef Tom Douglas is a cookbook author and owner of Etta's, Palace Kitchen, Dahlia Lounge, and the Dahlia Bakery. He also hosts the radio show Tom Douglas' Seattle Kitchen.

CHEF TOM DOUGLAS

GRILLED RIB STEAKS
WITH PANZANELLA

"This is a great way to eat a steak when you feel like firing up the grill on a beautiful summer day. The steak juices mingle with the grilled bread, vinaigrette, and vegetables for the most fantastic-tasting salad. Also try this recipe with grilled chicken instead of steak, or chunks of fresh mozzarella instead of goat cheese." Tom Douglas

The spice rub recipe makes enough for 4 large steaks; you may need to make only half a recipe.

Fire up the grill.

To make the spice rub: Combine ingredients in a small bowl.

To make the vinaigrette: Put the lemon juice in a bowl and whisk in the olive oil. Season with salt and pepper to taste. Set aside.

When you are ready to grill, brush the steaks lightly with olive oil. Pat the spice rub evenly over both sides of the steaks. Grill the steaks over direct heat, lid off, to desired doneness, turning often with tongs. (A 1-inch-thick steak will take about 8 minutes total for rare.)

Brush the bread with the olive oil and grill on both sides until golden and marked by the grill. Brush the onion slices with olive oil and grill on both sides until cooked and marked by the grill. Remove the steaks, bread, and onion from the grill and keep warm.

To make the panzanella, cut the grilled bread into bite-sized cubes. Separate the grilled onion into rings. Place the bread and onions in a large bowl and add the arugula, cucumber, and tomatoes. Add the vinaigrette and toss. Add the goat cheese and lightly toss again.

Divide the panzanella among 4 plates. Slice the steaks and place them over the salads. Garnish each salad with olives and serve immediately.

Makes 4 servings

Spice Rub

2 tablespoons kosher salt

1 teaspoon freshly ground black pepper

2 teaspoons paprika

1 teaspoon minced fresh rosemary

Vinaigrette

2 tablespoons lemon juice

1/3 cup extra-virgin olive oil

Kosher salt and freshly ground black pepper

Steaks

4 rib steaks, about 1 inch thick

Olive oil for grilling

4 1-inch-thick slices rustic bread

1 small red onion, peeled and cut in 3/4-inch slices

4 ounces small arugula leaves, washed and dried (about 4 to 6 cups loosely packed leaves)

1/3 English cucumber, thinly sliced into half-moons

1 generous cup cherry tomatoes, cut in half

4 ounces soft, fresh goat cheese, broken into chunks

20 olives, such as black oil-cured or kalamata

CHEF EMERIL LAGASSE
POMPANO
WITH CITRUS CRUST AND GRAPEFRUIT BUTTER SAUCE

It might take more than one BAM! to make this recipe, but it is well worth it. Emeril likes to make this with pompano—it is also good made with other mild-flavored white fish.

Makes 6 servings

Citrus Crust (recipe follows)

6 pompano fillets, skin on

1 to 1½ tablespoons Emeril's Essence, or other Creole seasoning

Grapefruit Butter Sauce (recipe follows)

Grapefruit zest in long curls, for garnish

Preheat oven to 375°F. Prepare the Citrus Crust.

Season the flesh side of the pompano with ½ to ¾ teaspoon Emeril's Essence per piece. Place the fillets skin side down on a nonstick rimmed baking sheet or buttered parchment paper. Divide the crust mixture evenly over the fillets and pat lightly into place.

Bake in preheated oven for about 20 to 25 minutes, or until fish is just done. Place fish on 6 warm plates and serve with Grapefruit Butter Sauce. Garnish with long curls of grapefruit zest.

Citrus Crust

1 teaspoon minced lemon zest

1 teaspoon minced lime zest

1 teaspoon minced orange zest

¾ cup dry, unseasoned bread crumbs

2 tablespoons butter, melted

1 tablespoon diced shallots

¼ teaspoon kosher salt

¼ teaspoon black pepper

1 teaspoon brown sugar

Blanch zest in boiling water for 1 minute and drain. Combine all ingredients in a mixing bowl and work with hands to combine.

Grapefruit Butter Sauce
Makes about ½ cup

½ cup sugar

1½ cups fresh grapefruit juice

¼ cup white wine vinegar

1½ tablespoons diced shallots

2 tablespoons heavy cream

12 tablespoons (1½ sticks) cold unsalted butter, cut into pieces

½ cup seedless grapefruit segments

Combine the sugar, juice, vinegar, and shallots in a small saucepan. Reduce over medium heat to ¼ cup. Mixture will foam up while reducing; watch closely and remove from and return to heat as needed to prevent boiling over.

Add cream and cook for 30 seconds more. Remove from heat. Gradually whisk in the butter, piece by piece. Add the grapefruit segments and stir gently to combine. Keep barely warm until ready to serve.

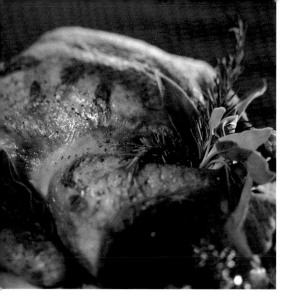

World champion professional tennis legend Andre Agassi is pictured here with his wife, Stefanie Graf, a retired professional tennis player and winner of 22 Grand Slam tournaments, and their two future tennis superstars, Jaden and Jaz Agassi. Being the competitive athlete that he is, Andre is equally competitive in the kitchen. After a few turkey fiascos and lots of practice, Andre finally came up with this perfected turkey recipe.

ANDRE AGASSI & STEFANIE GRAF

HERB ROAST TURKEY
WITH RED WINE CRANBERRY RELISH

Makes 8 to 16 servings, with leftovers

1 12- to 16-pound turkey

4 or more large fresh rosemary sprigs

1 large onion, skin on, quartered

1 head of garlic, broken apart

8 large sage leaves

1 tablespoon olive oil

1 tablespoon kosher salt

1/4 to 1/2 teaspoon freshly ground black pepper

Red Wine Cranberry Relish
Makes about 2 1/2 cups

3/4 cup red wine, such as Merlot or Syrah

1/2 cup finely chopped onion

1 tablespoon minced fresh ginger

1 large Gala apple, skin on, cored and cut in 1/4-inch dice

3 cups (12-ounce bag) fresh or frozen cranberries, chopped

1/2 cup orange juice

1 cup sugar

1/4 teaspoon ground cloves

1/4 teaspoon ground cinnamon

Allow 1½ hours' roasting time for a 12-pound turkey, and add about 5 to 10 minutes for each additional pound. This will be one of the most beautiful turkeys you've ever roasted!

Place an oven rack low in the oven. Preheat oven to 375°F.

Remove the giblets and neck from turkey cavities, checking that both cavities are empty. Rinse turkey with cold water, inside and out, and pat dry. Keep the legs tied together with the metal clip, or tie with butcher's twine.

Place half of the rosemary sprigs and all the onion and garlic in the bird's body cavity.

Pull the leaves off the remaining rosemary sprigs. Carefully loosen the turkey skin over the breast and legs (by running your hands under it), being careful not to tear it. Keeping them as flat as possible, tuck the sage leaves and the rosemary leaves you pulled off under the breast, thigh, and leg skin, arranging the herbs decoratively. Carefully pull the breast skin tightly down over the breast bone, then thread metal closure skewers through both sides of the skin flaps to bridge the turkey body cavity opening. Thread skewers alternately from left to right, then right to left. With a 12-inch piece of butcher's twine or white cotton string, work back and forth around the skewers to lace up the cavity, shoelace-style.

Spray a roasting rack with nonstick vegetable spray and place the turkey on the rack in an open, shallow roasting pan. Rub the turkey all over with the olive oil, then generously sprinkle with the salt and pepper.

Place the turkey on the low oven rack and roast until the inner, thickest part of the thigh registers 175°F. (Insert metal stem, instant-read thermometer in the back side of thigh by the turkey body.)

If you are cooking a larger turkey, you may need to tent the breast loosely with a piece of buttered foil to avoid overbrowning of the breast. About 30 to 45 minutes before the end of cooking, remove tent to allow browning.

When the turkey is done, remove from the oven. Before carving the turkey, let it stand for 10 to 15 minutes to allow the juices to settle. As the turkey stands, the thigh temperature will reach 180°F.

Use the pan drippings to make your gravy.

Red Wine Cranberry Relish
In a medium nonreactive saucepan, combine all ingredients. Bring to a simmer over medium-high heat, reduce heat, and simmer for about 30 to 35 minutes, until thickened and chutney-like in consistency. The mixture will thicken a little more after cooling. Serve with Herb Roast Turkey.

Best-selling cookbook author, chef, and food writer Sheila Lukins definitely gives us something to write about with this delicious swordfish recipe. She has received many awards for her contributions to the food world.

CHEF SHEILA LUKINS
SWORDFISH PROVENCAL

This dish makes for a wonderfully elegant outdoor feast during those beautiful summer evenings. Don't let the many ingredients scare you off—this recipe is worth every bit of slicing and dicing.

Makes 4 servings

1 large garlic clove, minced

Coarse salt

2½ tablespoons red wine vinegar

⅓ cup plus 2 tablespoons extra-virgin olive oil

Freshly ground black pepper

8 ounces tender green beans or haricots verts, ends snapped, halved diagonally

4 red new potatoes

½ cup ¼-inch-diced red bell pepper

½ small red onion, slivered lengthwise, rinsed in cold water, and drained thoroughly

¼ cup pitted Niçoise olives

1 tablespoon drained tiny capers

¼ cup loosely packed, slivered fresh basil leaves

2 tablespoons fresh lemon juice

4 (6 to 8 ounces each) swordfish steaks

1 hard-cooked egg, coarsely chopped

2 tablespoons chopped Italian parsley

In a large bowl, sprinkle the garlic with a generous pinch of salt and add the vinegar. Slowly drizzle in ⅓ cup of the olive oil, whisking constantly to make a vinaigrette. Season with pepper to taste and reserve.

Bring a pot of salted water to a boil. Have a large bowl of ice and water nearby. Place green beans in a strainer and plunge into the boiling water for 1 to 2 minutes to blanch. Immediately remove beans and drop them into ice water to stop the cooking. Drain thoroughly.

Cook the potatoes in boiling salted water until tender but not mushy, about 12 minutes. Drain. Slice the potatoes and place in another large bowl. Layer the green beans atop the potatoes, followed by the peppers, red onion, olives, capers, and basil. Do not toss until serving time.

Preheat the broiler or grill.

Meanwhile, combine the remaining 2 tablespoons of olive oil and the lemon juice in a bowl. Add the swordfish and coat well. Let marinate for 5 to 10 minutes.

Season fish with salt and pepper to taste. Place the fish in a lightly oiled broiler pan 4 inches from the heat source and broil for 4 minutes on the first side. Turn carefully and broil 4 minutes on the other side. Or oil grill lightly and grill fish until just done. Remove to the center of a large decorative platter.

Gently toss the reserved vegetables with the vinaigrette and arrange surrounding the swordfish. Sprinkle the chopped egg on top. Grind some pepper over all and garnish with chopped parsley.

Named one of the top 10 philanthropists in America, Paul G. Allen co-founded Microsoft with Bill Gates in 1976. Paul is the founder and chairman of Vulcan Inc., and chairman of Charter Communications. His many initiatives include the Experience Music Project in Seattle.

PAUL G. ALLEN
CHICKEN SAUTERNE

This recipe is one of Paul's favorite chicken dishes, and something his mother, Faye, has been making for years. Paul has fond memories of this simple but delightful dish from special occasions, family get-togethers and birthday dinners, from the time he was growing up all the way through today.

In a large saucepan, place chicken breasts in water to just cover and add 1 teaspoon of the salt. Simmer, covered, until tender (about 30 minutes). Remove skin and bones from chicken, leaving meat in large pieces. In a pan over high heat, reduce the chicken broth to 1 cup. Reserve.

Meanwhile, in a heavy skillet, melt 2 tablespoons butter. Add the mushrooms and sauté until tender. In the same pan, melt remaining butter, then stir in flour, onion, and seasonings. Whisk in reserved chicken broth, wine, and defrosted peas and onions. Cook, stirring constantly, over low heat until thickened. Then stir in the half-and-half and bring to a simmer. Cook, whisking, for 2 minutes, and then add the chicken. Heat until chicken is heated through. Salt to taste.

Makes 6 servings

3 whole chicken breasts with skin and bones

1 ½ teaspoons salt

5 tablespoons butter

1 cup thinly sliced mushrooms

3 tablespoons flour

1 tablespoon instant minced onion

½ teaspoon celery salt

½ teaspoon paprika

½ teaspoon dried mixed Italian herbs

½ teaspoon Worcestershire sauce

½ cup California Sauterne or other table wine

1 (9- to 16-ounce) package frozen peas with onions, defrosted and drained

1 cup half-and-half or light cream

Vocalist, pianist, composer, and actor Harry Connick, Jr., is an artist of wide-ranging talent. The three-time Grammy winner has also been nominated for the Tony, Emmy, Oscar, and Golden Globe awards.

Makes 6 to 8 servings

4 tablespoons (½ stick) butter

1 ½ cups chopped onion

1 cup chopped celery

1 large green bell pepper, chopped

1 pound boneless, skinless chicken thigh meat, cut in ½-inch pieces

3 tablespoons minced garlic

2 bay leaves

1 teaspoon dried thyme

1 teaspoon Creole seasoning

½ teaspoon ground cayenne

¼ cup tomato paste

1 pound andouille sausage or hot Italian sausage, cut in 1-inch pieces

2 (14.5-ounce) cans diced tomatoes in juice

2 (14.5-ounce) cans chicken broth

2 ½ cups long-grain white rice

1 cup diced, cooked ham

Salt and black pepper

HARRY CONNICK, JR.
JAMBALAYA

As he often does in his professional life, New Orleans native Harry Connick, Jr., shows he's in touch with his childhood roots with this traditional Creole dish.

In a large Dutch oven over medium-high heat, melt the butter. Add the onions, celery, and green pepper, and sauté until softened, about 3 minutes.

Add the chicken, garlic, and seasonings, and sauté about 2 minutes. Stir in the tomato paste, then add the sausage, and sauté about 2 minutes more.

Add the diced tomatoes with their juice, chicken broth, rice, and ham, and bring to a boil. Cover with a tight-fitting lid and reduce the heat to a simmer. Cook, covered, about 20 to 30 minutes more, or until rice is tender and liquid is absorbed. Check near the end of the cooking time and add a little water if more liquid is needed.

Remove bay leaves. Season liberally with salt and pepper. Serve with hot pepper sauce if desired.

PASTA & RISOTTO

Pasta is one of the most versatile dishes you can cook. It's great for a well-planned meal or a spur-of-the-moment dining delight. And with a noodle shape for every mood and personality, you can get expressive. Pasta recipes are varied and can be easy for the beginner cook or a challenge for the accomplished chef. If rice is more your grain, then the king of rice, risotto, is a delightful way to tempt your taste buds and your guests. The secret to perfect risotto is slow cooking and patient stirring.

Seafood Pasta—Lynne & Britney Spears   82

Spaghetti & Meatballs—Susan Lucci   84

Pasta Puttanesca—Ann Curry   86

**Pumpkin & Sage Risotto
with Mushroom and Pea Ragout**—Joan Lunden   88

Smoked Salmon Linguine—Tracy McGrady   90

**Lobster Ravioli
with Tomato Tarragon Cream Sauce**—Phil Mickelson   92

Vegetable Pasta—Minnie Mouse   93

Penne al Funghi Porcini—Pierce Brosnan   94

Baked Macaroni & Cheese—Steve Wariner   96

Makes 8 servings

16 tablespoons (2 sticks) butter

1 pound crawfish tails, peeled

1 pound shrimp, peeled

½ teaspoon black pepper

½ teaspoon cayenne pepper

4 teaspoons Old Bay Seasoning

2 bunches green onions, thinly sliced

10 tablespoons flour

1 quart half-and-half

¾ pound crabmeat

1 pound dry linguine

2 tablespoons extra-virgin olive oil

¼ teaspoon salt

Juice of ½ lemon

Lynne, mother of singing sensation Britney, took a personal role in the book and sent us handwritten instructions for this recipe. "Thank you both for your incredibly enthusiastic support." Tami Agassi

LYNNE & BRITNEY SPEARS
SEAFOOD PASTA

This rich and luscious recipe yields a dish that stays true to Lynne and Britney's Louisiana roots. They like to season the sauce with Tony Chachere's Creole Seasoning and liquid crab boil, if available, in place of the Old Bay Seasoning.

In a large, deep skillet or heavy Dutch oven, melt half the butter over medium-high heat. Add the crawfish and shrimp and sprinkle with black pepper, cayenne, and 2 teaspoons of the Old Bay. Sauté until three-quarters done, about 3 to 4 minutes, depending on the size of the shellfish. Take care not to overcook. Using a slotted spoon, remove seafood to a plate.

Melt the remaining butter in the pan, add the onions, and sauté about 1 minute. Add the flour and stir until blended. Whisk in half of the half-and-half and the remaining Old Bay. When smooth, whisk in the remaining half-and-half. Return shellfish to the sauce to finish cooking, and add the crabmeat to heat through.

Meanwhile, cook pasta in boiling salted water until just al dente. Drain. Toss pasta with olive oil, salt, and lemon juice.

Serve sauce over pasta.

When it comes to spaghetti and meatballs, Susan Lucci definitely wins the Emmy! An award-winning actor and the "woman you love to hate," Erica Kane on All My Children, Susan somehow finds time to cook between kidnappings, marriages, and plane crashes.

SUSAN LUCCI
SPAGHETTI & MEATBALLS

This sauce is scrumptious as is, or if you like, you can add a little red wine just before stirring in the tomato paste.

Makes 8 to 10 servings

Meatballs

1 pound ground round

½ pound ground veal

½ pound ground pork

¼ cup finely chopped onion

1 tablespoon dry bread crumbs

1 egg

1 tablespoon chopped fresh Italian parsley

1 ½ teaspoons dried oregano

1 ½ teaspoons dried basil

¼ teaspoon dried thyme

1 teaspoon salt

½ teaspoon black pepper

Sauce

¼ cup extra-virgin olive oil

½ cup finely chopped onion

4 to 6 garlic cloves, finely chopped

1 tablespoon dried oregano

1 ½ teaspoons dried basil

¼ teaspoon dried thyme

2 (6-ounce) cans tomato paste

2 (28-ounce) cans tomato purée

6 cups water

1 Knorr beef bouillon cube

2 teaspoons salt

¼ teaspoon black pepper

2 pounds dry spaghetti

Chopped parsley, for garnish

½ cup grated Parmesan cheese

To prepare meatballs: In a large mixing bowl, combine all meatball ingredients. Knead mixture all together, being careful not to overwork the meat. Roll mixture into 1 ½-inch balls.

To cook meatballs and make sauce: Heat oil in a 6- to 8-quart heavy metal pot over medium-high heat. Working in small batches, brown the meatballs in the oil, browning on all sides, about 7 to 8 minutes per batch. Remove from pot and set aside on a plate.

In the same pot, sauté the ½ cup onions and the garlic until glazed but not browned. Stir in herbs and immediately add the tomato paste so that the seasonings do not burn. Then add the tomato purée. Add 5 cups of the water. Drop in bouillon cube. Stir from the bottom of the pot.

Bring the sauce to a boil, then reduce to a simmer. Cover the pot, making sure you do not close the lid too tight; leave a small opening for sauce to breathe. Simmer for ½ hour, stirring frequently. Add meatballs and remaining cup of water if needed. Re-cover pot, leaving space for sauce to breathe, and continue cooking for 20 to 30 minutes, stirring frequently. Season with the salt and pepper.

Meanwhile, in another large pot, bring 4 to 5 quarts of salted water to a rapid boil. Add a little olive oil to the water so spaghetti does not stick.

When water is boiling rapidly, put in spaghetti, and stir frequently. Do not cover or leave unattended. Cook until al dente, approximately 10 to 12 minutes, or according to package directions.

Drain spaghetti in a colander and place in a large bowl. Mix in a ladleful of sauce and toss lightly.

Place spaghetti on plates with 2 meatballs per serving. Add more sauce, garnish with parsley, and serve with grated cheese.

1 bunch fresh basil

2 tablespoons minced garlic, about 1 head

1 ½ cups high-quality extra-virgin olive oil

1 cup pitted Greek kalamata olives, coarsely chopped

2 cups halved cherry tomatoes or chopped vine-ripened tomatoes

1 (2-ounce) tube anchovy paste

1 pound dry, small shell, gigli, orecchiette, or torchio pasta

Freshly grated Parmesan cheese

ANN CURRY
PASTA PUTTANESCA

"I usually hand-pit Mediterranean black olives for this dish. Cherry tomatoes are best, but Romas work, too. The key is to pick a flavorful type. Shell pasta is best because it catches the sauce, which is so good you want a lot of it." Ann Curry

Pick the leaves from the basil, rinse, and spin thoroughly in a salad spinner or spread on paper towels to dry. When dry, slice through the leaves once, and reserve.

In a medium bowl, mix the garlic, olive oil, and kalamata olives. (I like to smoosh the olives with my fingers to bring out the flavor.)

Add the tomatoes, anchovy paste, and basil leaves. Let sit for at least 30 minutes to let the flavors mellow.

When ready to serve, cook the pasta in boiling salted water just until al dente. Drain. Toss the sauce with the cooked pasta and sprinkle generously with Parmesan cheese.

Serve with French or Italian bread to sop up the sauce. Enjoy!

Emmy Award-winner Ann Curry is a news anchor for NBC and contributing reporter for Dateline NBC. *Ann, shown here with her sister, Jean Hodson, was one of the first celebrities to say yes to this project. "She interviewed me once, and I found her to be one of the most beautiful and gracious women I have ever met." Tami Agassi*

JOAN LUNDEN
PUMPKIN & SAGE RISOTTO
WITH MUSHROOM AND PEA RAGOUT

This recipe is from Joan's book Growing Up Healthy, *which she co-authored with Dr. Myron Winick. While you might not greet the day with this delicious dish, it's perfect for prime time.*

To make the risotto: In a large saucepan, stir together 6 cups broth and canned pumpkin. Bring to a boil, reduce the heat, and hold at a very low simmer.

Meanwhile, in a 4-quart Dutch oven, heat oil over medium heat and sauté onion for about 5 minutes, or until tender. Add fresh pumpkin or squash and cook for 2 minutes, stirring.

Add rice, stirring for 2 minutes more.

Add wine to rice mixture and cook until the wine has evaporated. Slowly add 2 cups of the broth mixture, stirring constantly. Continue to cook and stir until liquid is absorbed. Add the remaining broth mixture, ¾ cup at a time, stirring constantly until the broth is absorbed (about 30 minutes). Stir the Parmesan cheese and sage into the rice mixture. Season to taste with black pepper.

Meanwhile, to make the ragout: Heat oil in a nonstick 10-inch skillet over medium heat and sauté onion until tender and golden, about 10 minutes. Add garlic and cook 30 seconds. Stir in mushrooms; increase heat to medium-high and cook 5 minutes, or until mushrooms are wilted. Stir in peas and broth, and cook until heated through. Serve about ½-cup portion in the center of each bowl of risotto.

Makes 6 to 8 servings

6 cups reduced-sodium chicken broth

½ cup canned pumpkin

1 tablespoon olive oil

1 small onion, finely chopped

3 cups cubed, peeled pumpkin or butternut squash

2 cups Arborio rice

⅓ cup dry white wine, or substitute reduced-sodium chicken broth

½ cup grated Parmesan cheese

2 teaspoons chopped fresh sage

Black pepper

Mushroom and Pea Ragout

1 tablespoon olive oil

1 small onion or shallot, chopped

1 small garlic clove, crushed

8 ounces mixed exotic or wild mushrooms

1 (10-ounce) package frozen peas, thawed and drained

¼ cup reduced-sodium chicken broth

Tracy McGrady, NBA All-Star and MVP candidate from Orlando Magic, makes a slam dunk with this recipe.

Makes 4 to 6 servings

1 pound dry linguine

2 tablespoons olive oil

1 cup thinly sliced mushrooms

1 tablespoon minced garlic

¼ teaspoon crushed red pepper flakes

½ cup clam juice

¼ cup lemon juice

1 tablespoon lemon zest

¼ cup white wine

1 cup cream

2 cups thinly bias-cut raw asparagus

¾ cup matchstick-cut red bell peppers

6 to 8 ounces smoked salmon, cut in thin slices or flaked

Salt and black pepper

2 tablespoons thinly sliced chives

1 tablespoon chopped parsley

TRACY McGRADY
SMOKED SALMON LINGUINE

This is an All-Star pasta dish with a luxurious silkiness that belies its simplicity. To keep the cost down, ask your fishmonger for lox trim.

Right before making the sauce, cook the pasta according to package directions, until just al dente. Drain it well, toss very lightly with a splash of olive oil and salt to taste, then cover and keep warm.

To make the sauce: Heat the 2 tablespoons olive oil in a large sauté pan over medium-high heat. Add the mushrooms and sauté until lightly browned, about 2 minutes.

Add the garlic and pepper flakes, and sauté 30 seconds more. Add the clam juice, lemon juice, zest, and wine, and cook until the sauce is reduced by half, about 3 minutes.

Whisk in the cream, then add asparagus and bell peppers, and bring sauce to a quick boil to thicken. Add the smoked salmon and cooked pasta, then season with salt and pepper to taste. Cover and let heat through.

Place pasta on a large platter and sprinkle with the herbs.

PHIL MICKELSON

LOBSTER RAVIOLI
WITH TOMATO TARRAGON CREAM SAUCE

This recipe is from Chef David, the Mickelson family chef. He makes his own pasta with semolina flour, but you can substitute purchased high-quality fresh pasta for convenience.

Prepare Lobster Filling first.

Cut pasta sheets into 24 squares, approximately 4 inches on a side. Unless actively being worked with, keep pasta covered with plastic wrap to keep dough moist while you fill the ravioli.

To make the ravioli: Lay out a pasta square on a clean, dry work surface. Brush outer inch of pasta square with a little beaten egg on all four sides. Place about 2 tablespoons filling in center, then place a second pasta square over filling. With your fingers, gently fit top pasta square around the filling, snugging it close to the filling to eliminate all air pockets. Press pasta down firmly, then crimp with a fork to seal ravioli securely on all four sides.

Cover filled ravioli with plastic wrap to prevent drying out. Repeat ravioli-making process with remaining dough and filling. You should have 12 large ravioli. Keep ravioli covered until ready to cook. (If made ahead, cover and refrigerate.)

Cook ravioli right before serving. In a large pot over high heat, bring 6 to 8 quarts lightly salted water to a boil. Add 2 teaspoons olive oil. With the water at a low boil, add 4 to 6 ravioli, one at a time, to the water. Return the heat to high and cook ravioli until pasta is done, about 10 minutes. Keep the water at a boil, but do not let it boil so hard as to break the ravioli. Repeat cooking procedure until all ravioli are cooked, topping up boiling water and adding a little more oil as needed. As ravioli are done, remove with a slotted spoon and keep warm.

Divide ravioli among large, heated plates, and spoon Tomato Tarragon Cream Sauce over, dividing evenly. Sprinkle with minced fresh herbs if desired.

Lobster Filling
Steam lobster tails over boiling water for 10 minutes. When cool enough to handle, remove meat from shells and finely chop lobster meat. Mix in chervil, vanilla, salt, and pepper. Refrigerate, covered, until needed.

Tomato Tarragon Cream Sauce
In a heavy saucepan over medium-high heat, heat oil and sauté onion until translucent. Add cream, tarragon sprigs, and nutmeg, and cook until cream is reduced by half.

Remove tarragon, and add tomatoes and tomato paste. Simmer over medium heat until reduced by one-quarter. Purée until smooth. Strain, and season with salt and pepper to taste. Keep warm for service.

Makes 4 servings

1 pound fresh pasta sheets

1 egg, beaten

Lobster Filling (recipe follows)

Olive oil

Tomato Tarragon Cream Sauce (recipe follows)

Minced fresh tarragon or chervil, optional

Lobster Filling

2 (8-ounce each) frozen lobster tails, defrosted

1 tablespoon chopped fresh chervil or, if not available, substitute chopped fresh tarragon

1 teaspoon vanilla extract

½ teaspoon salt

¼ teaspoon black pepper

Tomato Tarragon Cream Sauce
Makes about 2¼ cups

1 tablespoon olive oil

½ cup chopped sweet onion

2 cups heavy whipping cream

2 sprigs fresh tarragon

⅛ teaspoon freshly ground nutmeg

1 (14.5-ounce) can Italian tomatoes

¼ cup tomato paste

¼ teaspoon salt

⅛ teaspoon black pepper

MINNIE MOUSE
VEGETABLE PASTA

This pasta is an enchanted vegetable wonderland. Minnie loves to serve it to Mickey when they visit Minnie's Country House in the Magic Kingdom Park.

Makes 6 to 8 servings

1 pound dry penne pasta

⅓ cup olive oil

2 cups small broccoli florets

2 cups sliced mushrooms

1 yellow squash, cut in thin matchstick strips

3 garlic cloves, minced

1 shallot, minced

⅓ cup dry white wine

2 ripe tomatoes, chopped

½ cup homemade or high-quality store-bought basil pesto

1 ½ teaspoons salt

¼ teaspoon cracked black peppercorns

½ cup freshly shredded Parmesan cheese

In a large pot of boiling salted water, cook the pasta according to package directions, or until al dente. Drain.

Meanwhile, in a deep 12-inch skillet, heat the olive oil over medium-high heat until hot but not smoking. Add the broccoli, mushrooms, squash, garlic, and shallot, and cook, stirring, for 4 to 5 minutes, or until the vegetables are just tender.

Add the white wine and cook until the liquid is reduced by half. Stir in the tomatoes, pesto, salt, and pepper. Stir in cooked pasta and cook, stirring, for 2 minutes, or until heated through. Toss in half the cheese.

Transfer the pasta to serving plates and sprinkle with remaining cheese. Serve immediately.

Tami,
This is my favorite recipe!
Love, Minnie

The object of Mickey's affection, Minnie has been with Mickey since 1928. "Michael Eisner, CEO of The Walt Disney Company, sent me this framed picture of Minnie. It hangs prominently on my office wall and I absolutely adore it." Tami Agassi

Actor Pierce Brosnan loves this dish as much as James Bond loves his leading ladies. It's a recipe worthy of a 007 rating.

Makes 4 servings

¼ cup high-quality extra-virgin olive oil

4 fresh porcini mushrooms, sliced

1 garlic clove, minced

¼ cup chopped Italian parsley

Salt and black pepper

½ cup white wine

1 cup chopped peeled tomatoes, liquid drained

1 pound dry penne pasta—we like to use DeCecco brand

2 tablespoons grated Parmigiano-Reggiano cheese, plus more for passing

PIERCE BROSNAN
PENNE AL FUNGHI PORCINI

This is a recipe from Pierce's favorite Santa Monica restaurant, Il Ristorante di Giorgio Baldi. Seasonal, meaty-textured wild porcini mushrooms, botanical name Boletus edulis, *can be found in farmers markets. Look for them also under the names* cèpes, Steinpilz, *or just* boletes.

Heat the oil in a large skillet over medium-high heat, and sauté the sliced porcini mushrooms with the garlic and parsley. Season with salt and pepper.

Add the wine and let everything simmer until the wine evaporates. Add the tomatoes and cook for 4 to 5 minutes.

Meanwhile, boil the penne until al dente. Drain the pasta and add it to the sauce together with the grated cheese. Let cook for 2 minutes at low heat. Taste for seasoning.

Serve very hot. Pass extra cheese for sprinkling.

Steve has been making records for over 25 years. He is an award-winning singer, songwriter, guitar player, and producer. In addition to his own long list of hits, including "Holes in the Floor of Heaven" and "Kansas City Lights," Steve has written hit songs for others, including Garth Brooks' "Longneck Bottle" and Clint Black's "Nothin' But the Taillights."

Makes 6 servings

1 (7-ounce) package
or 2 cups dry wagon wheel pasta

2 tablespoons butter

2 tablespoons flour

2 teaspoons dry mustard

2 teaspoons salt

¼ teaspoon pepper

2½ cups whole milk

⅓ cup beer

2 cups (8 ounces) shredded medium
or sharp Cheddar cheese

1 medium tomato, thinly sliced

STEVE WARINER
BAKED MACARONI & CHEESE

The beer adds a unique and delicious flavor—whether you pour it from a longneck bottle or an aluminum can.

Preheat oven to 375°F. Grease a 2-quart shallow baking dish.

Cook pasta according to package instructions and drain well.

In a saucepan over medium-high heat, melt butter, then stir in flour, mustard, salt, and pepper. Gradually whisk in milk and then beer. Bring to a simmer, and cook and stir until mixture thickens slightly.

Remove from the heat and add 1½ cups of the cheese. Stir until melted. Stir in cooked pasta. Pour pasta into the prepared baking dish. Top with remaining cheese and then tomato slices.

Bake 20 to 25 minutes, or until bubbly.

COMFORTS, SNACKS
& FAVORITES

We all have flavor memories that bring back a time when we felt happy, loved, or taken care of. Maybe it's a recipe our grandmother made or a dish our mom offered when we were feeling down and out—comfort foods often take us to our childhood. Years later, eating those foods can give us a culinary hug when we need it, and making those recipes is a good way to pass the memories along to others. Share the love.

Classic Pot Roast with Caramelized Onion Gravy—Robin Williams — 100

Mexican Dinner—Clint Black — 102

Shepherd's Pie—Elizabeth Hurley — 104

Almond Chicken Salad—Alice Cooper — 106

King Ranch Chicken—George Strait — 107

Beef Stroganoff—Kelly Preston — 108

Zelma's Hungarian Stuffed Cabbage—Libby Pataki — 110

Dump Chili—Venus Williams — 111

Chicken Sauerkraut—Quincy Jones — 112

Chicken & Dumplings—Tim McGraw — 114

Faggots & Mushy Peas with Mint—Tom Jones — 116

Heirloom Tomato Sandwich with Gorgonzola Aioli on Focaccia—Tony Danza — 118

Tuna Sandwich—Scott Hamilton — 120

Actor and comedian Robin Williams, pictured here with personal chef John Mathies, is notorious for not knowing how to cook. "When Robin's wife, Marsha Garces Williams, called to say he would participate in the book, she mentioned that it would be funny to submit a recipe for the only two things Robin can make—a cup of coffee and a bowl of cereal. They had their chef submit a recipe instead. This is one of Robin's favorite dishes." Tami Agassi

ROBIN WILLIAMS

CLASSIC POT ROAST
WITH CARAMELIZED ONION GRAVY

Created by Robin's personal chef, John Mathies, this roast is meltingly delicious. Serve with oven-roasted root vegetables, buttered noodles, rice, or mashed potatoes.

Preheat oven to 325°F. Trim beef of excess fat; if necessary, cut into four even pieces to fit better in your cooking vessel. Season meat with salt and pepper.

Heat oil in a large, deep pan or Dutch oven over high heat until hot but not smoking. Brown meat well on all sides, about 2 to 3 minutes per side, and remove to a plate when done.

Turn down heat to medium-high; add onions and sauté until well browned and caramelized, scraping up all the browned bits from the pan. Add wine, broth, tomato paste, garlic, vegetables, and bay leaves. Return meat to the pan, and bring to a boil.

Cover and place in preheated oven. Cook until meat is very tender, about 2 to 3 hours. Halfway through cooking, turn meat over so all surfaces spend time in the liquid.

When done, remove from oven, discard bay leaves, and remove celery and carrot with a slotted spoon to a dish; reserve. Take meat from pot, and keep warm. Mix up the flour and water to make a smooth slurry. Whisking constantly, drizzle slurry into the sauce and bring to a boil. Reduce the heat, and simmer sauce 3 to 5 minutes to thicken and cook out flour taste. Adjust the seasoning.

Serve pot roast sliced, with vegetables and gravy.

Makes 8 servings

1 (5-pound) boneless chuck roast

2 teaspoons salt

½ teaspoon black pepper

2 tablespoons olive oil

3 onions, diced

½ cup red wine

½ cup beef broth

2 tablespoons tomato paste

2 garlic cloves, crushed

2 carrots, cut in large chunks

2 stalks celery, cut in large chunks

2 bay leaves

3 tablespoons flour

¼ cup water

CLINT BLACK & LISA HARTMAN-BLACK

MEXICAN DINNER

Put yourself in Clint's shoes and whip up these yummy low-fat "fajitas." They'll definitely put you in a great State of Mind.

To make the fresh salsa: Combine chopped tomatoes, jalapeño, half the lime juice, and half the cilantro; set aside.

Marinate chicken in remaining lime juice and cilantro for at least 20 minutes or up to 1 hour.

Spray a large nonstick sauté pan with nonstick vegetable spray and heat over medium-high heat. Add onions and peppers and sauté in batches until tender. Keep warm.

Heat a grill. Season chicken breasts with salt and pepper to taste, and grill for approximately 5 minutes on each side, or until cooked through. Slice into strips.

Serve with warm corn tortillas, sour cream, and reserved salsa.

Clint Black is an award-winning country singer and songwriter. Lisa Hartman-Black is an accomplished actor and vocalist.

Actor, model, and producer Elizabeth Hurley is not just another pretty face. She cooks up a mean shepherd's pie.

ELIZABETH HURLEY
SHEPHERD'S PIE

Makes 6 to 8 servings

Potato Topping

4 large russet potatoes (about 2 ½ pounds), peeled and cut into quarters

4 tablespoons (½ stick) butter

¾ cup milk, warmed

1 teaspoon salt

¼ teaspoon black pepper

1 tablespoon olive oil

1 large onion, chopped (about 2 ½ cups)

4 large carrots, diced (about 2 ½ cups)

2 pounds ground lamb

1 teaspoon minced fresh rosemary

½ cup red wine

2 tablespoons tomato paste

Salt and black pepper

2 tablespoons cornstarch

1 ½ cups lamb, chicken, or vegetable stock, or canned low-sodium chicken or vegetable broth

"This is my all-time favourite recipe, which was taught to me by my father. I usually serve it with a large green salad." Elizabeth Hurley

First make the potato topping: Place potatoes in a medium pot and cover with cold water. Bring to a boil over high heat, then reduce heat and simmer potatoes until soft. Drain them thoroughly and then mash them ferociously with the butter, milk, salt, and plenty of black pepper. Set aside.

Place an oven rack in top third of oven. Preheat oven to 400°F.

Meanwhile, heat olive oil in a large skillet and gently fry the onion and carrots until tender, about 4 to 5 minutes. Remove with a slotted spoon and reserve.

In the same skillet, add the raw lamb, quickly stirring with a wooden spoon so that most of the meat can get seared by hot fat. After about 4 to 6 minutes, add the rosemary, wine, and tomato paste. Mix in and stir up all the browned bits. Season to taste with a good pinch of salt and some freshly ground pepper. Bring lamb mixture to a boil.

Meanwhile, whisk the cornstarch into the lamb stock. When lamb mixture comes to a boil, stir stock mixture into lamb. Stirring constantly, cook for about 1 minute to thicken broth. Taste and add more salt and pepper if you think it's needed.

Transfer the lamb mixture to a 9-by-13-inch baking dish. Spoon the mashed potatoes on top. Make furrows in the top of the potatoes with a fork.

Bake the dish at the top of the preheated oven for about 20 minutes, or until the top is brown and crispy and lamb is bubbling.

Makes 6 to 8 entrée servings

1 lemon

8 cooked boneless, skinless chicken breast halves

1 bunch seedless green grapes, stemmed and halved lengthwise

1 bunch green onions, finely chopped

Salt and black pepper

1 ¼ cups mayonnaise

1 ½ tablespoons butter

1 cup slivered blanched almonds

⅔ cup sugar

An unforgettable shock-rocker, Alice Cooper sticks to tradition with this tasty salad. Alice is pictured here with his wife, Sheryl, in their kitchen.

ALICE & SHERYL COOPER
ALMOND CHICKEN SALAD

Legendary rock n' roller Alice Cooper is a classic and so is his recipe: no mascara needed.

Grate zest from lemon, juice the lemon, and reserve separately.

Cut chicken into bite-sized pieces. In a large bowl, combine chicken, lemon zest, grapes, and onions. Season with salt and pepper to taste.

Mix lemon juice into mayonnaise, then mix into salad to moisten evenly.

In a nonstick skillet over medium heat, melt butter. Add almonds and mix well. Sprinkle sugar evenly over almonds and continue to mix until evenly coated. Increase heat to medium-high and, stirring constantly, cook until almonds begin to brown and sugar begins to caramelize. Spread almonds on a clean, dry baking sheet. When almonds are cool and crisp, break up the clumps.

Mix almonds into salad. Adjust seasoning as needed.

Makes 6 to 8 servings

1 (10.75-ounce) can condensed cream of chicken soup

1 (10.75-ounce) can condensed cream of mushroom soup

¾ cup chicken broth

½ of 10-ounce can Ro-Tel Tomatoes and Green Chiles

6 boneless, skinless chicken breast halves, cut in strips

8 8-inch corn tortillas, cut into 6 pieces each

1 onion, chopped

½ pound Cheddar cheese, shredded

Strait from the Heart and into your mouth, country music legend and Lone Star native George Strait knows how to cook it up.

GEORGE STRAIT
KING RANCH CHICKEN

If you're from Texas, this famous recipe certainly needs no introduction! Since you're likely to have most of the ingredients on hand, this dish can be your Ace in the Hole in case extra cowboys drop by. We're sure you'll agree that this dish packs a flavor as big as Texas.

Preheat oven to 350°F.

Mix together first 4 ingredients and set aside.

Grease a 9-by-13-inch baking dish. Spread chicken evenly in pan. Cover with tortilla pieces, overlapping in a shingle-like fashion. Spread onion evenly over tortillas. Pour reserved soup mixture overall. Top with cheese.

Bake for 1 hour, or until mixture is bubbly.

Kelly Preston is an actor and model, wife of John Travolta, and mother of two.

Makes 8 servings

6 tablespoons flour

1 teaspoon salt

½ teaspoon black pepper

1 ½ pounds beef sirloin, cut in ¼-inch-thick strips, fat trimmed

¼ cup vegetable oil

1 large onion, chopped

3 cups sliced fresh mushrooms

2 teaspoons minced garlic

1 (14-ounce) can reduced-sodium beef broth

1 teaspoon paprika

1 tablespoon Worcestershire sauce

2 cups sour cream

Egg noodles, cooked

Chopped parsley, for garnish

KELLY PRESTON
BEEF STROGANOFF

If you wish to add red wine to the recipe, mix it into the broth before stirring into the sauce. You can also make this recipe with chicken breast as an alternative to the beef.

In a bowl, or a paper or plastic bag, mix ¼ cup of the flour, salt, and pepper. Shake meat in the seasoned flour to coat evenly.

Heat 1 tablespoon of the oil in a large, heavy skillet over medium-high heat. Add the onion and mushrooms, and sauté for about 5 minutes. Remove from the pan with a slotted spoon, and reserve.

Add 2 tablespoons more oil to the pan and raise the heat to medium-high to high. When oil is hot, shake the excess flour from the beef, separating the pieces. Brown half of the beef, turning continuously, for about 3 minutes; remove. Add the remaining oil and brown the remaining beef; remove.

Add the garlic to the pan and sauté for ½ minute. Whisk the remaining 2 tablespoons flour into the drippings, add the broth, and stir until smooth and thick, scraping up all the browned bits. Add the paprika and Worcestershire. Correct the seasoning with salt and pepper to taste. Bring to a simmer, then stir in the sour cream. Whisk until smooth, and return meat and mushrooms to the sauce to heat through.

Serve with egg noodles and garnish with chopped parsley.

LIBBY PATAKI

ZELMA'S HUNGARIAN STUFFED CABBAGE

First Lady Libby Pataki, wife of Governor George Pataki of New York, loves to make this family tradition for her husband. Pataki's recipe has been adapted for today's busy cook; this slow-cooker version can be turned on and forgotten about while you go off to work or play.

Makes about 4 to 6 servings

1 small (2-pound) head green cabbage

3¼ cups water

½ cup rice

1 tablespoon olive oil

½ cup chopped onions

2 tablespoons minced garlic

½ pound ground pork

½ pound ground beef

⅓ cup golden raisins

1 teaspoon salt

¼ teaspoon pepper

2 (8-ounce) cans tomato sauce

2 tablespoons sugar

3 tablespoons cider vinegar

2 cups sauerkraut, rinsed and drained

1 cup sour cream

Cut core from the cabbage and place in a deep pot. Add water to cover. Remove cabbage and set aside. Bring water to a full boil. Carefully place cabbage in the water, reduce heat to low, and cover the pot. As each leaf softens, remove it and let cool.

Meanwhile, in a medium saucepan, bring 3 cups of the measured water to a boil. Stir in rice and parboil for 10 minutes. Drain well.

Heat oil in a skillet over medium-high heat. Sauté onions for 2 to 4 minutes, or until lightly browned. Stir in garlic. Remove from heat. Mix onion and garlic into drained rice, then mix in pork, beef, raisins, salt, and pepper.

Place about ¼ cup of the mixture in each cabbage leaf, fold in the sides, roll up the leaf, and pin with a toothpick. As you get down to the smaller cabbage leaves, use 2 leaves for each roll. You should get about 12 rolls.

Mix together tomato sauce, remaining ¼ cup water, sugar, and vinegar.

Spread about ¼ cup sauce in the bottom of the slow-cooker. Add a layer of sauerkraut, then a layer of cabbage rolls, closely packed. Repeat until all cabbage rolls and sauerkraut are used, ending with sauerkraut.

Pour remaining tomato sauce on top of the cabbage rolls. Set cooker on low heat and cook for 8 to 10 hours.

Carefully remove cabbage rolls from slow-cooker, then remove toothpicks. Serve cabbage rolls hot. Pass sour cream for topping.

Makes 8 servings

2 pounds ground beef or ground turkey
(if using ground turkey, add ½ cup olive oil)

2 large onions, chopped

1 large green bell pepper, chopped

8 to 10 garlic cloves, chopped

6 jalapeño peppers, seeded if desired, and chopped

9 tablespoons chili powder

2 tablespoons paprika

2 tablespoons ground cumin

Lawry's Seasoned Salt or sea salt

3 (14.5-ounce) cans Del Monte Stewed Tomatoes,
Mexican Recipe

2 (16-ounce) cans kidney beans, rinsed and drained

3 cups water

Tennis star Venus Williams has won numerous tennis titles, including the U.S. Open and Wimbledon. It's clear that Venus knows how to serve it up in more ways than one!

VENUS WILLIAMS
DUMP CHILI

It's healthy and Grand Slam easy!

In a Dutch oven or other large, heavy pan, mix beef or turkey with the onions, bell pepper, garlic, jalapeños, chili powder, paprika, and cumin. Add seasoning salt to taste. Place over medium heat and cook all together until meat is completely cooked and vegetables are tender.

Purée tomatoes in a blender for 10 to 20 seconds. Add tomatoes, beans, and water to chili, and cook on low heat for 2 hours. Stir periodically when it starts to boil. Serve over Fritos or alone.

Music impresario Quincy Jones is noted for his work as a film composer, activist, and TV producer. He is also the all-time most nominated Grammy artist. We were ecstatic when Quincy personally called to tell us he would love to submit this recipe. Quincy is pictured here with his daughter, Kenya Jones.

QUINCY JONES
CHICKEN SAUERKRAUT

Makes 6 servings

1 chicken, cut up (6 to 8 pieces)

Salt and black pepper

1 tablespoon olive oil

6 red potatoes, quartered

1 onion, sliced

4 garlic cloves, crushed

1 (24-ounce) jar sauerkraut, drained

1 cup chicken stock or reduced-sodium canned chicken broth

Quincy likes to use Spike Seasoning in this recipe. Although it doesn't call for browning the chicken, if you have time, you certainly could do so. Brown it in the olive oil before proceeding with the recipe.

Preheat oven to 400°F. Season chicken with salt and pepper to taste.

Coat a Dutch oven with the oil. Arrange the chicken on the bottom of the pan. Add the potatoes, onion, garlic, and drained sauerkraut. Top with lots of freshly ground black pepper. Pour the chicken stock over all the ingredients.

Bring to a boil, then cover pot. Place in the preheated oven to bake for 40 minutes. Remove the lid, and cook about 20 minutes more, or until potatoes are completely tender, chicken juices run clear, and sauerkraut is slightly browned in some places.

He likes it, he loves it, he wants some more of it! And who wouldn't? This recipe is another hit single from award-winning country music star Tim McGraw.

TIM McGRAW
CHICKEN & DUMPLINGS

Make this old-fashioned supper dish with a large natural or organic chicken for flavorful results.

In a large, heavy soup pot or Dutch oven, place chicken, quartered onion, celery stalks, garlic, herbs, cloves, salt, peppercorns, and water. Bring to a boil over medium-high heat, then reduce the heat, cover, and simmer until chicken falls from the bones, about 1 hour. (Note: If you happen to be lucky enough to get a true stewing hen, it may take 2 ½ to 3 hours to become tender, and you'll have lots of great flavor.)

Remove chicken to cool and drain. Strain the broth, pressing firmly on solids to extract the liquid. Let broth settle, then skim excess fat. Reserve broth.

Meanwhile, when chicken is cool enough to handle, tear the meat into bite-sized pieces and reserve; discard the skin and bones.

Melt butter in the soup pot, and whisk in 2 tablespoons flour until smooth. Cook over medium heat, stirring constantly, for 3 minutes. Whisk reserved broth into butter and flour mixture, and continue whisking vigorously until sauce comes to a boil and no lumps remain. Add chopped onion, diced carrots and celery, and reserved chicken. Whisk in bouillon cubes and let sauce reduce by half.

In a small bowl, mix cornstarch with ¼ cup cold water. Whisk the slurry into the sauce and return to a boil to thicken. Taste and adjust the seasoning.

To make the dumplings: In a large bowl, quickly mix dumpling ingredients until just combined, to make a loose dough. Thin with water if needed. Do not overmix. With a ¼-cup measure, drop scant quarter-cupfuls of batter into the simmering liquid. Cover and cook WITHOUT PEEKING for about 15 to 20 minutes, or until fluffy and cooked through.

Stir in peas and chopped fresh herbs. Serve immediately.

Makes 8 servings

1 whole (4- to 5-pound) chicken, a stewing hen if available

1 onion, quartered

2 stalks celery, cut in chunks

3 garlic cloves, crushed

2 sprigs fresh parsley

1 teaspoon dried whole thyme

½ teaspoon dried sage

1 bay leaf

2 cloves

1 teaspoon salt

1 tablespoon black peppercorns or ½ teaspoon ground black pepper

3 quarts water

2 tablespoons butter

2 tablespoons flour

1 cup chopped onion

2 carrots, diced

1 cup diced celery

2 chicken bouillon cubes

¼ cup cornstarch

¼ cup cold water

2 cups frozen sweet peas, defrosted and drained

¼ cup mixed chopped fresh herbs, such as parsley, dill, and thyme

Dumplings

2 cups flour

1 tablespoon baking powder

½ teaspoon salt

¼ cup minced green onion

¼ cup minced fresh parsley

1 egg, beaten

1 cup milk

Singer, songwriter, and entertainer Tom Jones is a legend, not to mention a lady-killer. Tom knows what he likes, and he loves these faggots and mushy peas.

TOM JONES
FAGGOTS & MUSHY PEAS
WITH MINT

Makes 4 servings

Faggots

2 tablespoons butter

½ cup finely chopped white onion

4 garlic cloves, minced

1 pound ground fresh pork

1 tablespoon very finely minced fresh sage

¼ teaspoon ground nutmeg

1 ½ teaspoons salt

¼ teaspoon black pepper

1 egg

½ cup dry bread crumbs

½ pound fresh pork liver, cut in chunks

Mushy Peas with Mint

2 tablespoons butter

1 large shallot, minced

1 (10-ounce) box frozen peas, defrosted and drained well

½ cup chicken broth

1 tablespoon chopped fresh mint

Salt and black pepper

This is a traditional British comfort dish. Faggots are a form of meatball, but typically made of pork and pork liver.

Preheat oven to 375°F.

To make the faggots: Melt the butter in a nonstick skillet over medium-high heat. Add the onions and sauté 2 to 3 minutes. Add the garlic and sauté 30 seconds more.

In a large bowl, combine the onions, ground pork, seasonings, egg, and bread crumbs. Using clean hands, mix well.

Place the liver in a food processor and pulse for about 30 seconds, until finely chopped; or dice liver very fine. Mix liver into pork mixture.

Using a ¼-cup measure, scoop up mixture and shape into 12 meatballs. As balls are shaped, place them, spaced apart, on a rimmed baking pan. Bake in preheated oven for about 20 minutes, or until just done. Take care not to overcook.

Meanwhile, make the peas: Melt the butter in a nonstick skillet over medium-high heat, add the shallot, and sauté 1 minute. Add the drained peas and sauté 2 minutes more. Add the broth and cook until peas are very tender and almost all liquid has evaporated but peas are still a little juicy, about 3 minutes.

Stir in the mint, remove from the heat, and mash with a potato masher. Season with salt and pepper to taste. Keep warm.

Serve faggots immediately with the mushy peas.

Makes 4 sandwiches

2 teaspoons very finely minced garlic

¼ cup high-quality mayonnaise

3 tablespoons crumbled
Gorgonzola cheese

4 (3- by 4-inch) squares focaccia bread,
sliced open

4 large heirloom tomatoes,
a mixture of varieties and colors

1 ½ tablespoons extra-virgin olive oil

1 tablespoon balsamic vinegar

1 tablespoon chopped fresh basil

1 ½ cups baby arugula leaves, washed and
spun dry

Kosher salt and fresh-ground
black pepper

Actor and performer Tony Danza is the
Boss in his kitchen when whipping up
this tasty sandwich for friends.

TONY DANZA
HEIRLOOM TOMATO SANDWICH
WITH GORGONZOLA AIOLI ON FOCACCIA

Also delicious with slices of fresh mozzarella cheese and crisp pancetta, for the ultimate Italian BLT.

Preheat broiler or grill.

In a small bowl, mash the garlic, mayonnaise, and Gorgonzola together until well combined. Set aside.

Under the broiler or on a hot grill, toast the cut sides of the focaccia until lightly golden.

Meanwhile, slice the tomatoes about ½ inch thick.

In a medium bowl, whisk together the oil, vinegar, and basil, and then toss in the arugula.

Spread the top layer of the focaccia with the Gorgonzola aioli. Place the tomato slices on the bottom pieces of focaccia, dividing them evenly among the sandwiches. Sprinkle liberally with salt and pepper, then top with the dressed arugula. Close the sandwiches and serve immediately.

TUNA SANDWICH

Scott enjoys a mean grilled tuna sandwich. It'll have your family doing back flips! If you're a sweet gherkin fan instead of a dill lover, then go ahead and substitute.

Makes 4 sandwiches

8 slices hearty bread

1 tablespoon butter, softened

2 (6-ounce) cans albacore tuna, drained very well

6 tablespoons mayonnaise

6 tablespoons finely chopped dill pickle

1 tablespoon capers, chopped

¼ cup finely chopped celery

1½ teaspoons chopped fresh dill

3 tablespoons finely chopped green onion

¼ teaspoon kosher salt

¼ teaspoon black pepper

¾ cup coarsely grated sharp Cheddar cheese

Spread each piece of bread very lightly on one side with the butter. Place on a cookie sheet and cover with plastic wrap. Set aside.

In a large bowl, combine the tuna with the mayonnaise, then add all the remaining ingredients but the cheese and stir until very well combined. Fold in the cheese.

Divide the tuna mixture evenly among 4 slices of the bread, spreading the mixture on the unbuttered side. Top with 4 remaining slices of bread, buttered side up.

Meanwhile, heat a grill to medium-high or place a grill-pan over a burner on medium-high heat. Grill sandwiches for approximately 2 to 3 minutes per side, or until bread is toasty.

Professional figure skater Scott Hamilton is a four-time U.S. Champion, four-time World Champion, 1984 Olympic Champion, and world-class good guy. Scott is pictured here with his wife, Tracie, and their son, Aiden.

SIDES, ACCOMPANIMENTS
& BREAKFAST

Breakfast is the meal that starts your day and serves as liaison to the rest of your sunlit hours. While we tend to stick to basics—eggs, toast, bacon, and cereal—a little creativity can bring a welcome change and be a nice way to shake you out of a rut. Breakfast is noted as the most important meal of the day, but the side or accompaniment to a meal is also essential. After all, it's pretty much a date for the main dish. And you wouldn't want to set up your entrée with an incompatible side, would you? Be it baked beans, rice, or grilled veggies, sides and accompaniments are the tasty secret to a well-composed meal.

Grandma Grant's Banana Nut Bread—Amy Grant 124

Toast—Joan Rivers 126

Thanksgiving Sweet Potato Casserole—Chelsea Clinton 128

Baked Beans—Michael R. Bloomberg 130

Benihana Fried Rice—Chef Rocky H. Aoki 131

Glazed Turnips—Tori Amos 132

Grilled Summer Vegetables—Mia Hamm 134

Cornbread with Honey Glaze—Mark Curry 136

Dutch Babies—Beverly Sills 138

Crispy Brown-Sugared Bacon Strips—Arnold Palmer 140

Rae's Noodle Kugel—Howard Schultz 142

Rosemary Mashed Potatoes—Dr. Phil McGraw 143

Makes 1 loaf

8 tablespoons (1 stick) butter, softened

1 cup sugar

2 eggs

3 bananas, sliced (about 2 cups)

1 teaspoon baking soda

2 cups flour

¼ teaspoon salt

½ cup chopped pecans

Amy Grant is a Grammy Award-winning singer, songwriter, performer and noted humanitarian.

AMY GRANT

GRANDMA GRANT'S BANANA NUT BREAD

This wonderful recipe was Amy's Grandmother Grant's. Since it calls for sliced bananas instead of the usual purée, there's no need to wait for the fruit to become overripe—you can make a loaf anytime you're in the mood to bake! When a couple of days old, banana bread is delicious sliced and toasted.

Grease an 8½-by-4½-inch loaf pan.

Cream the butter with sugar. Mix in eggs, bananas, baking soda, flour, salt, and pecans. Pour into the prepared pan.

Place in cold oven. Heat oven to 300°F and cook for about 1½ hours, or until loaf tests done.

Cool for 5 minutes on a rack. Then remove from pan and let cool completely, right side up.

"This recipe has been in my family for generations." Joan Rivers

Makes 2 servings
2 slices white bread*
Butter or margarine

JOAN RIVERS
TOAST

We toast comedienne Joan Rivers for her culinary honesty. Joan prefers white bread, but you can use whole grain, as we did.

Take the 2 slices of white bread and place them in a toaster. Press down the toaster handle. Wait 2 minutes, or until the toast pops up.

After removing toast from the toaster, spread with butter or margarine to taste.

*For holidays and special occasions, raisin bread may be substituted. For these special occasions we call it "Joan Rivers' Holiday Toast."

CHELSEA CLINTON
THANKSGIVING SWEET POTATO CASSEROLE

Chelsea says, "This is a traditional Thanksgiving dish in the Clinton family." We think it's fluffilicious!

Makes 10 to 12 servings

5 cups mashed cooked sweet potatoes

8 tablespoons (1 stick) butter, melted

½ cup milk

1 cup granulated sugar

½ teaspoon vanilla extract

2 eggs, well beaten

Topping

1 cup brown sugar

2 cups mini-marshmallows

5 tablespoons butter, melted

Preheat oven to 350°F. Grease 1 or more baking dishes (recipe fills to top a deep 9-by-13-inch dish) and reserve.

In a large bowl, mix together mashed sweet potatoes, ½ cup melted butter, milk, granulated sugar, vanilla extract, and eggs. Spread sweet potatoes in baking dish.

To make the topping: In a small bowl, mix together brown sugar and marshmallows. Sprinkle mixture on top of sweet potatoes. Drizzle remaining melted butter over marshmallow topping.

Bake until sweet potatoes are heated through and topping is puffy and browned.

Michael R. Bloomberg is mayor of the City of New York and founder of Bloomberg L.P., a financial news information company.

MICHAEL R. BLOOMBERG
BAKED BEANS

Makes 8 to 10 servings

3 16-ounce cans B&M baked beans

1 cup molasses

6 strips bacon (about 6 ounces), cut into thirds

Salt and pepper

French's Classic Yellow mustard

Mayor Bloomberg grew up in a suburb of Boston, a.k.a. Beantown. This is his favorite baked beans recipe, and if you've never made baked beans, let this be your success story.

Preheat oven to 300°F.

In a bowl, mix beans and molasses until well combined. Pour half of the mixture into a 9-inch glass pie dish. Top with 6 pieces of bacon. Pour in remaining beans and top with remaining 12 pieces of bacon.

Bake in preheated oven for 2 hours.

Add salt, pepper, and French's mustard to taste.

Rocky Aoki first came to the USA as a wrestler. He went on to become a hugely successful business tycoon and restaurateur extraordinaire. Today, Rocky has 50 award-winning restaurants across the nation and is the author of 11 best-selling books.

CHEF ROCKY H. AOKI
BENIHANA FRIED RICE

Flecked with colorful vegetables, this recipe is quick and easy to make. It's a great way to use up your leftover take-out rice!

Heat a 12-inch nonstick skillet or wok over medium heat. Add 1 teaspoon oil and scramble the eggs until just firm. Remove from the pan and let cool; then chop the eggs and reserve.

Meanwhile, add the remaining 1 tablespoon oil to the pan, and raise the heat to medium-high. Sauté the onion, green onion, and carrots until tender, about 2 to 3 minutes. Mix in the rice, chicken, and chopped eggs. Add the sesame seeds, salt, and pepper, stirring well. Add the butter and soy sauce to the mixture, stirring until well combined.

Makes about 8 servings

4 teaspoons peanut or other vegetable oil

2 eggs, beaten

2 tablespoons chopped onion

2 tablespoons chopped green onion

2 tablespoons chopped carrots

4 cups steamed white rice

1 cup chopped cooked chicken

1 teaspoon sesame seeds

¾ teaspoon salt, optional

¼ teaspoon black pepper

2 tablespoons butter

4 teaspoons soy sauce

2 pounds young turnips, peeled,
then halved, quartered, or cut in finger-size
sticks, depending on size

4 tablespoons butter

Sea or kosher salt

Freshly ground black pepper

2 tablespoons of your favorite honey

½ to ¾ cup water

Chopped fresh basil, for garnish

TORI AMOS
GLAZED TURNIPS

Tori loves the Glazed Turnips that her personal chef, Duncan Pickford, makes for her. Duncan likes to tourne *(turn or shape with a knife) the turnips into little barrel shapes.*

Place turnips in a large, heavy pan and add butter, salt and pepper to taste, honey, and water.

Cut a round of baking parchment to fit exactly over the turnips—or place a lid on slightly askew.

Bring liquid to a boil over medium heat and then turn down to medium-low. Cook for about 20 minutes, or until the water has reduced to a thick, shiny glaze in the bottom of the pan and the turnips are tender.

Place the turnips in a serving dish and spoon the glaze over.

Garnish with a little chopped fresh basil and serve.

Tori Amos is a musician, singer, and songwriter. You'll find these turnips as poetic as her lyrics.

Makes 6 servings

Lemon Thyme Vinaigrette (recipe follows)

1 zucchini, cut in ½-inch-thick long diagonal slices

1 yellow crookneck squash, cut in ½-inch-thick long diagonal slices

1 large eggplant, cut crosswise into ½-inch-thick rounds

1 large red bell pepper, cut lengthwise into 6 wedges and seeded

1 red onion, peeled and sliced crosswise into ⅓- to ½-inch-thick rounds

Olive oil

Kosher salt

Cracked black pepper

Lemon Thyme Vinaigrette

1 ½ teaspoons very finely minced lemon zest

1 teaspoon very finely minced fresh thyme

1 teaspoon very finely minced garlic

1 teaspoon Dijon mustard

1 tablespoon fresh lemon juice

¼ cup olive oil

A professional soccer player, Mia is the world's leading scorer and the most recognized female soccer player in the world.

MIA HAMM
GRILLED SUMMER VEGETABLES

The next time you're firing up the grill, don't limit yourself to grilling just the main course. These vegetables will take full advantage of the live fire, too.

Get the fire going in the grill. You want to start grilling the vegetables over pretty hot coals.

Meanwhile, make the Lemon Thyme Vinaigrette, and reserve.

Lay out vegetables on a baking sheet and drizzle or brush with olive oil. Turn vegetable slices and drizzle again.

Place the vegetables over very hot coals and grill for about 1 to 3 minutes on each side to mark nicely.

Move vegetables to a cooler area of the grill and cook, turning occasionally, until just done to your taste. Allow about 3 to 4 minutes total for the bell pepper; about 4 to 6 minutes for the zucchini and yellow squash; about 6 to 8 minutes for the eggplant and onion. For the firmer vegetables, you may want to cover them loosely with foil or the grill lid for a few minutes of the cooking time so the center gets tender.

As vegetables are done, remove from the grill and sprinkle with salt and pepper to taste. Drizzle generously with the Lemon Thyme Vinaigrette.

Lemon Thyme Vinaigrette

Whisk all ingredients together, gradually drizzling in the oil at the end and whisking until emulsified.

Mark Curry is an accomplished actor and comedian. If you're ever Hangin' with Mr. Cooper, *you'll want to try this irresistible cornbread.*

MARK CURRY

CORNBREAD

WITH HONEY GLAZE

Makes one 8-inch round

Cornbread

1 cup flour

1 cup yellow or white cornmeal

2½ teaspoons double-acting baking powder

½ cup chopped toasted pecans

2 tablespoons sugar

¾ teaspoon salt

¼ teaspoon cayenne pepper

1 egg, lightly beaten

1 cup milk

¼ cup corn oil

Glaze

2 tablespoons honey

2 tablespoons butter, melted

The toasted pecans and honey glaze make this quick bread a standout.

Preheat oven to 425°F. Spray an 8-inch cake pan with nonstick vegetable spray.

In a large bowl, stir together flour, cornmeal, baking powder, pecans, sugar, salt, and cayenne. Reserve.

In another large bowl, whisk together the egg, milk, and oil. Stir the cornmeal mixture into the milk mixture until just combined well but not overmixed.

Spoon the batter into the baking pan and smooth out the top with a rubber spatula.

Bake in preheated oven about 12 to 15 minutes, or until golden and a cake tester inserted in the center comes out clean. Remove from oven.

Meanwhile, in a microwave-safe container, combine the glaze ingredients. Microwave for about 30 seconds, or until melted. Immediately brush over the hot cornbread.

Cut in wedges. Serve warm.

BEVERLY SILLS
DUTCH BABIES

This is a favorite late-night, after-performance snack or Sunday brunch treat.

Makes 1 or 2 servings

3 eggs

½ cup flour

½ cup milk

½ teaspoon salt

3 tablespoons butter, melted

Place an 8-inch cast-iron or other heavy, ovenproof skillet in freezer while preparing batter. Preheat oven to 450°F.

In a blender, mix the eggs, flour, milk, and salt on low speed.

Remove skillet from freezer and smear it with the melted butter to coat bottom and sides of pan.

Pour in batter, and bake in preheated oven for about 20 minutes, or until puffed and browned.

Serve with jam, stewed fruit, maple syrup, or butter.

Chairwoman of the Metropolitan Opera and former chairwoman of Lincoln Center for the Performing Arts, Beverly Sills, "America's Queen of Opera," sings the praises of these Dutch Babies.

Hall of Fame pro golfer and highly successful business executive Arnold Palmer's recipe is a great way to swing into breakfast.

Makes 4 to 6 servings
1 pound sliced bacon, at room temperature
1 cup packed brown sugar

ARNOLD PALMER
CRISPY BROWN-SUGARED BACON STRIPS

You can use either thin- or thick-sliced bacon for this recipe. Arnold often makes the recipe ahead, then stores the bacon in aluminum foil and just reheats it to serve.

Preheat oven to 350°F.

Roll (or pat or shake) raw bacon in brown sugar, and place strips on a rack set on a flat pan with sides.

Bake bacon in preheated oven for about 25 to 30 minutes, or until dark brown. You can turn the bacon over once with tongs.

When bacon is well done, remove with tongs and drain on brown paper very thoroughly. As it cools, the bacon will harden, and it can then be broken into smaller pieces or served whole.

Ultimate entrepreneur and Starbucks coffee mogul Howard Schultz brews up a world-class noodle dish with his traditional kugel.

HOWARD SCHULTZ
RAE'S NOODLE KUGEL

"Despite the sweetness of the kugel, this is a side dish, not a dessert, quite often served during the Yom Kippur Break the Fast." Howard Schultz

Makes 8 to 10 servings

8 ounces dry flat egg noodles, cooked

4 tablespoons (½ stick) butter, melted

1 cup cream-style, small-curd cottage cheese

2 large eggs, beaten

½ cup sugar

1 teaspoon ground cinnamon, or more as desired

½ teaspoon salt

3 tablespoons sour cream

½ cup golden raisins, or more as desired

¼ cup heavy cream

1 teaspoon vanilla extract, optional

Preheat oven to 350°F.

Mix all ingredients together with cooked noodles. Pour into a buttered 8-inch square pan or glass pie dish. Bake for 35 to 45 minutes, or until light golden brown.

Recipe can be doubled and put in a larger baking dish.

Named one of the "Most Intriguing People of 2002" by People *magazine, Dr. Phil has influenced millions of people to "get real" about their behavior and create a more positive life. His television show,* Dr. Phil, *has been making headlines since its September 2002 launch, when it received the highest ratings of any new syndicated show since the debut of* The Oprah Winfrey Show *16 years earlier. Dr. Phil has also endeavored to link good food and good health, and generously shares a special recipe from his latest cookbook with us.*

DR. PHIL McGRAW
ROSEMARY MASHED POTATOES

This true comfort food is transformed into a healthy side dish by using fat-free sour cream or fat-free evaporated milk. Fresh rosemary gives these mashed potatoes such a wonderful taste that you definitely won't miss the gravy.

Place the broth and rosemary in a small saucepan set over high heat. Bring the mixture to a simmer, cover, remove from heat, and set aside.

Place the potatoes in a large saucepan and cover with cool water to a depth of 2 inches. Bring to a boil over high heat. Partially cover, reduce the heat to medium-low, and simmer until potatoes are tender, about 15 minutes. Drain.

Place the potatoes in a large bowl and mash with a potato masher or an electric mixer at medium speed. Beat in the rosemary and broth mixture, then beat in the sour cream or evaporated milk, mustard, and salt. Spoon into a medium bowl and garnish with the paprika or ground black pepper before serving.

Makes 8 servings

⅔ cup no-salt, fat-free chicken or vegetable broth

2 tablespoons fresh rosemary, chopped

6 large baking potatoes, preferably russet, peeled and cut into 1-inch pieces

⅓ cup fat-free sour cream, at room temperature, or ⅓ cup fat-free evaporated milk

2 teaspoons Dijon mustard

½ teaspoon salt

Sweet paprika or freshly ground black pepper

SWEETS, DESSERTS & OTHER INDULGENCES

"While visions of sugarplums danced in their heads…" Dessert is usually the last tasty morsel to delight your tongue after a great meal and leaves a lip-smackin' lasting impression. And who doesn't like dessert? Dessert recipes are the most commonly passed around and shared through generations, families, and friends. From old-fashioned pies, fluffy cakes, and fresh baked cookies to fruit parfaits and liqueur-laced chocolate mousses, dessert is a special way to end a day or just treat yourself!

Sweet Potato Pie—Alonzo Mourning	146
Apple Pie—Anastacia	148
Chocolate Mousse Parfaits—Dyan Cannon	150
Rustic Roasted Pears & Grapes—Chef Lidia Bastianich	152
Strawberry Cornmeal Shortcakes—Chef Tom Douglas	154
Wahiawa Pineapple Cheesecake with Macadamia Nut Crust—Chef Sam Choy	156
Bento Box—Chef Nobuyuki Matsuhisa	158
Warm Blackberry Whipped Egg Custard—Chef Graham Kerr	160
Raspberry Cream Cheese Brownies—Ray Romano	162
Oatmeal Cake—Jack & Barbara Nicklaus	163

ALONZO MOURNING
SWEET POTATO PIE

This family recipe is a nice ending to any holiday lineup.

Makes two 9-inch pies, serving 12 to 16

3 (about 2½ pounds total) sweet potatoes, boiled until soft, then peeled (4 cups puréed)

12 tablespoons (1½ sticks) butter or margarine, softened

1½ cups sugar

¼ teaspoon salt

6 eggs

1 teaspoon lemon extract

2 tablespoons vanilla extract

2¼ teaspoons ground cinnamon

¼ teaspoon ground nutmeg

1 (12-ounce) can evaporated milk (not sweetened condensed milk)

2 deep-dish 9-inch pie crusts

Preheat oven to 425°F.

Place sweet potatoes and butter in a mixing bowl and beat on medium speed until combined. Add remaining ingredients except pie crusts, and mix on medium speed until smooth. Divide mixture between pie crusts.

Bake in preheated oven for approximately 15 minutes. Then reduce the heat to 350°F and continue baking about 40 minutes more, or until a knife inserted midway between center and rim of pan comes out clean and pies are golden brown on top.

Place pies on a rack to cool.

Alonzo Mourning, retired NBA basketball star and New Jersey Net, clears the court with this tasty dish. It'll be dribblin' down your chin! Pictured with his mother, Julia Hadnot.

Makes one 9-inch pie, serving 6 to 8

Topping

3 tablespoons butter, cold

⅓ cup flour

⅓ cup brown sugar

1 teaspoon ground cinnamon

Pie

¾ cup sugar

2 tablespoons flour

⅛ teaspoon salt

1 egg, beaten

½ teaspoon vanilla extract

1 cup sour cream

2 cups ½-inch-diced green apples

1 frozen 9-inch pie shell

Anastacia is a professional singer, songwriter, and performer, and a breast cancer activist.

ANASTACIA

APPLE PIE

You can bake this early in the morning and refrigerate it until dinner. If you use Granny Smith apples, the tart fruit, delicate custard, and crispy buttery topping make a delightful sweet-and-tangy contrast.

Preheat oven to 400°F.

Prepare the topping: Cut the butter into small pieces, then add the remaining topping ingredients. Stir slightly to coat butter pieces with dry ingredients. Refrigerate, covered, until ready to use.

To make the pie: Stir dry ingredients together and set aside.

In a large bowl, mix the egg, vanilla, and sour cream. Mix wet and dry ingredients together. Add the apples, and pour the mixture into the pie shell.

Bake in preheated oven for 20 minutes. Remove pie from oven and sprinkle evenly with topping. Return pie to oven for about 25 minutes, until topping appears to be melted and slightly crispy.

Cool thoroughly before cutting. Store refrigerated.

Dyan Cannon and friends. Acclaimed Oscar-nominated actor Dyan Cannon is known for her work both on and off camera. Here is a little something she has worked up in the kitchen.

DYAN CANNON

CHOCOLATE MOUSSE PARFAITS

Silky smooth and soooo chocolaty, this dessert will win high praise from your fans. Dyan sometimes piles the mousse into a baked pie shell and serves it up as a luscious pie.

To make crumbs: Mix melted butter and crumbled cookies. Reserve.

To make filling: Melt chocolate and amaretto together in a double boiler. Remove from heat and whisk to blend. Add egg yolks to chocolate mixture and whisk in.

Beat egg whites until stiff; fold into chocolate mixture.

Whip the cream until it forms stiff peaks, then fold into chocolate mixture.

To assemble the parfaits: In each of 12 parfait glasses, place about ¼ cup filling. Sprinkle with 1 ½ tablespoons cookie crumb mixture. Repeat 3 more times, ending with crumbs. Chill until ready to serve.

Makes 12 servings

Crumbs

4 tablespoons (½ stick) butter, melted

10 to 12 Oreo cookies or ½ (9-ounce) package chocolate wafers, broken up in blender or food processor, or by hand

Filling

12 ounces semisweet chocolate morsels

½ cup amaretto

6 eggs, separated

2 pints whipping cream

Makes 6 servings

2 cups seedless red grapes

1 cup sugar

⅔ cup Moscato or other fruity sweet
white wine

Juice of 2 lemons

2 tablespoons apricot jam

½ vanilla bean, split lengthwise

3 ripe but firm Bosc pears

CHEF LIDIA BASTIANICH

RUSTIC ROASTED PEARS & GRAPES

This recipe would be delicious spooned over vanilla bean ice cream or polenta pound cake.

Preheat oven to 375°F. Place the grapes in a 9-by-13-inch baking dish.

Stir the sugar, Moscato, lemon juice, apricot jam, and vanilla bean together in a bowl until blended. Pour over the grapes. Cut the pears in half through the core and remove the stems, cores, and seeds. Quarter the pears if very large. Nestle the pears, cut side up, into the grapes.

Bake, uncovered, for 30 minutes, then turn pears cut side down. Continue baking until the pears are tender and the liquid around the grapes is thick and syrupy, about 20 to 30 minutes. Remove the pears and let stand until the pan syrup thickens, about 10 minutes. If thicker syrup is desired, carefully remove grapes as well. Place syrup in a small saucepan and reduce over medium heat to desired consistency.

Serve the pears hot or warm, with some of the grapes and their pan syrup spooned around them.

A cookbook author and star of Lidia's Italian-American Kitchen *and* Lidia's Italian Table, *Lidia Bastianich is pictured here getting creative in her own kitchen.*

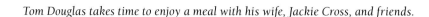

Tom Douglas takes time to enjoy a meal with his wife, Jackie Cross, and friends.

CHEF TOM DOUGLAS
STRAWBERRY CORNMEAL SHORTCAKES

Makes 6 servings

Cornmeal Shortcakes

2 cups flour

½ cup yellow cornmeal

⅓ cup sugar, plus more for sprinkling

1 tablespoon baking powder

8 tablespoons (1 stick) cold butter, cut in small pieces

1 teaspoon vanilla extract

1 cup heavy cream

1 egg white, slightly beaten

1 quart strawberries, hulled and sliced

¼ to ⅓ cup sugar, as needed

Sweetened whipped cream

"Washington strawberries have a short, unpredictable season, but amazing flavor. When available, use fragrant local berries to fill these shortcakes. Puréeing a small amount of the berries makes them juicy, and a little cornmeal gives the buttery, tender biscuits some crunch and texture." Tom Douglas

To make the cornmeal shortcakes: Preheat oven to 425°F.

In a bowl, combine the flour, cornmeal, ⅓ cup sugar, and baking powder. Using a pastry blender, your fingers, or two forks, cut in the cold butter until mixture is crumbly like a coarse cornmeal. Mix vanilla into cream, then pour into flour mixture. Mix with a rubber spatula or fork until just combined.

Turn the dough onto a lightly floured work surface and use a rolling pin to roll dough about ¾ inch thick. With a round cutter, cut into shortcakes about 3½ inches in diameter.

Place the shortcakes on a parchment-lined baking sheet set in another baking sheet. (This double-pan method slows the browning of the bottoms until the shortcakes are cooked through.) Brush each shortcake with a little beaten egg white and sprinkle lightly with sugar.

Bake in preheated oven until golden and cooked through, about 20 to 30 minutes.

Meanwhile, combine the strawberries with the sugar, depending on the sweetness of the berries. Transfer about 1 cup of the sweetened berries to a blender or food processor and purée. Mix the purée back into the sliced berries.

Cut the shortcakes in half horizontally. Fill each shortcake with strawberries and whipped cream, and replace top. Serve immediately.

Sam Choy is an award-winning restaurateur, best-selling cookbook author, and United Airlines celebrity chef. He has many restaurants that bear his name, including ones in Tokyo, Guam, and San Diego.

CHEF SAM CHOY

WAHIAWA PINEAPPLE CHEESECAKE

WITH MACADAMIA NUT CRUST

Famed Hawaiian chef Sam Choy surfs in with this tropical cheesecake, made extra-moist with fresh fruit. Macadamia nuts make an unusual, rich crust.

Preheat oven to 350°F.

To make the crust: In a food processor combine all the crust ingredients and process to a coarse-meal consistency.

Grease a 9-inch springform pan. Pack the crust in the bottom of the pan and bake in preheated oven for 7 to 10 minutes, or until very lightly browned. Cool to room temperature. Leave oven on.

Meanwhile, make the filling: Cream the cream cheese, sugar, zests, and cornstarch together in a power mixer or food processor. Add the sour cream, eggs, and rum, one ingredient at a time, mixing well and scraping down the bowl before adding the next ingredient.

In a towel, squeeze some of the juice out of the pineapple. Pour half the filling on top of the prebaked, cooled crust. Stir the pineapple into the rest of the batter. Pour into the cake pan and smooth the top.

Now it's time to make the caramel swirl in the cake. Using a spoon, drizzle caramel sauce in a swirl on top of the cake batter. (If necessary, gently warm caramel sauce in microwave until just spoonable consistency.) To achieve more of a swirl, use the tip of a knife to gently swirl the caramel.

Bake for about 1 1/2 to 1 3/4 hours, or until edges are firm but center 2 inches of cheesecake still moves slightly when pan is shaken. Cool and then refrigerate overnight before serving. To serve, run a small sharp knife around pan sides to loosen cake, then carefully remove sides of springform pan. Slice with a knife dipped in hot water.

Serve with additional caramel sauce if desired.

Makes one 9-inch cheesecake, serving 12

Crust

1 cup macadamia nuts

1/4 cup sugar

3 tablespoons butter, melted

2 tablespoons flour

Filling

24 ounces cream cheese, softened

1 1/4 cups granulated sugar

1 teaspoon minced orange zest, optional

1 teaspoon minced lemon zest, optional

1/4 cup cornstarch

1 1/2 cups sour cream

5 eggs

1 tablespoon Myers's dark rum

2 cups small-diced fresh pineapple, drained

1/4 cup homemade or high-quality purchased caramel sauce

Nobu Matsuhisa is an acclaimed chef and restaurateur, with Nobu and Matsuhisa restaurants around the globe.

CHEF NOBUYUKI MATSUHISA
BENTO BOX

Makes 4 servings
Chocolate Soufflés

4 eggs, separated

5 tablespoons plus 2 teaspoons sugar

1 ½ teaspoons cornstarch

4 ½ ounces semisweet chocolate, preferably about 70% cacao solids, chopped, or about ¾ cup semisweet chocolate chips

5 tablespoons unsalted butter

Shiso Syrup

2 (2-inch-diameter) shiso leaves,* or substitute 2 tablespoons coarsely chopped mint or basil

¼ cup water

4 ½ tablespoons sugar

Scant tablespoon mizuame,* or substitute light corn syrup

Sesame Toffee

4 ½ tablespoons sugar

1 tablespoon water

1 tablespoon white sesame seeds, toasted

1 tablespoon black sesame seeds, toasted

Sesame Ice Cream

½ cup plus 1 tablespoon sugar

4 egg yolks

¼ cup white sesame paste*

1 cup milk

1 cup heavy cream

Garnishes

Confectioners' sugar

Fruit, such as cherries and star fruit (carambola), or other seasonal fruit

Method for Chocolate Soufflés Preheat oven to 375°F. Butter six ½-cup soufflé cups and set aside.

In a mixer, whip the egg yolks, 2 tablespoons plus 2 teaspoons sugar, and cornstarch until mixture doubles in volume. Melt the chocolate and butter in a double boiler. In a clean bowl, whip egg whites and remaining sugar until soft peaks form. Fold egg yolk mixture into chocolate mixture. Carefully fold beaten egg whites into chocolate batter. Divide batter among the baking cups, filling ¾ full. Bake soufflés for approximately 15 minutes, or until set but centers are still very soft. Let cool for 3 to 4 minutes, then run a knife blade around the sides of the baking cups. Turn the soufflés out, and place them right side up on individual plates or in Japanese *jubako bento* boxes. Make and serve the soufflés quickly, otherwise the chocolate will harden.

Method for Shiso Syrup Prepare ahead. Briefly dip the shiso leaves in boiling water, then plunge into iced water and pat dry with a paper towel. Chop the leaves finely. Bring the other ingredients to a boil in a small saucepan. Boil for 2 minutes over medium heat. When the syrup thickens slightly, add the finely chopped shiso leaves and let the syrup cool.

Raspberry sauce or any tart sauce is also a good match for the chocolate soufflé.

Method for Nobu-Style Sesame Ice Cream Prepare ahead.
Make the toffee: Mix the sugar and water in a small saucepan and boil over medium heat until the syrup turns a light caramel color. Add the sesame seeds. Mix well with a wooden spatula. Spread mixture out thinly on a baking sheet and leave to cool at room temperature. Once hardened, break up toffee into small pieces.

Make the ice cream: Whisk together the sugar, egg yolks, and white sesame paste in a medium bowl and set aside. Heat the milk in top section of a double boiler until it boils. Add the sugar-egg-sesame mixture and place over, but not touching, simmering water. Cook, stirring, until mixture reaches 175°F. Then strain it quickly into a medium bowl and set aside to cool. Mix in the fresh cream, and complete the preparation by churning in an ice-cream maker according to manufacturer's instructions. Just before the ice cream sets, add the sesame toffee.

To Serve For each serving, arrange a chocolate soufflé and a scoopful of ice cream in a Japanese jubako bento box or on a large dessert plate. Sift confectioners' sugar through a sieve over the soufflés. Add the fruit and serve with the shiso syrup on the side. The syrup should be poured over the soufflés before eating.

*Look for shiso leaves, mizuame, and white sesame paste at stores that are well stocked with Japanese food products.

This spectacular and elaborate recipe breaks down into a number of easy steps. Only the actual baking of the soufflés must be done at the last minute. Prepare everything else ahead of time, and you'll wow your guests as surely as this world-renowned chef does. If you don't have bento boxes, this looks stunning on a decorative glass plate. Be sure to read through the entire recipe before you start.

An internationally known culinary and television personality, Graham Kerr is also an award-winning author.

CHEF GRAHAM KERR
WARM BLACKBERRY WHIPPED EGG CUSTARD

"The Italian people have a delicious dessert called zabaglione. It's a frothy egg yolk custard liberally laced with a sweet dessert wine. This is my version." Graham Kerr

Makes 8 servings

1 pound fresh, or frozen and thawed, blackberries

1¾ cups de-alcoholized fruity white wine

3 tablespoons real maple syrup

¼ teaspoon almond extract

¼ teaspoon vanilla extract

2 tablespoons cornstarch

½ cup sugar

1 cup Egg Beaters

Divide 1¼ cups of the blackberries among 8 large wine glasses. Press the rest of the blackberries through a sieve. Discard the seeds and set the purée aside.

Bring 1½ cups of the wine to a boil in a saucepan. Add the maple syrup, almond extract, and vanilla extract. In a small bowl, mix cornstarch into remaining wine to make a slurry. Whisk slurry into the boiling wine, bring back to a boil, and stir for 30 seconds while it thickens. Set aside to cool slightly.

Heat a small amount of water in another saucepan. Set a round copper or other metal bowl on top to create a double boiler. Reduce the heat to a simmer. Pour the sugar and Egg Beaters into the bowl and beat over the simmering water until frothy, thick, creamy, and more than tripled in volume, 3 minutes.

Pour the wine syrup into the egg mixture in a thin stream, whisking all the time. Add three-quarters of the blackberry purée, mixing well. Spoon the pudding over the blackberries in the glasses. Swirl the remaining purée on top of each dessert.

Makes 24 brownies

Brownie

16 tablespoons (2 sticks) butter

1 cup cocoa powder

1 cup sugar

1 (10-ounce) jar all-fruit seedless raspberry preserves (¾ cup)

4 eggs

1 teaspoon vanilla extract or ½ teaspoon almond extract

1 ¼ cups flour

¼ teaspoon baking soda

Swirl Topping

1 (8-ounce) package cream cheese

⅓ cup sugar

1 egg

½ teaspoon vanilla extract or ¼ teaspoon almond extract

1 cup raspberries

½ cup sliced almonds, optional

Comedian, actor, and star of Everybody Loves Raymond, *Ray Romano doesn't make any jokes about a great brownie. These are seriously delicious!*

RAY ROMANO
RASPBERRY CREAM CHEESE BROWNIES

Preheat oven to 325°F. Lightly spray a 9-by-13-inch glass baking dish with nonstick vegetable spray.

In a 2- to 3-quart heavy saucepan, melt the butter over medium heat. Whisk in the cocoa and cook till bubbling. Remove from heat and whisk in the sugar and preserves. Mix in the eggs and vanilla, blending thoroughly.

In a small bowl, stir together flour and baking soda, then add to chocolate mixture, stirring until fully incorporated. Pour into baking dish and smooth the top.

Then mix the swirl topping: Beat together the cream cheese, sugar, egg, and vanilla. Fold in raspberries.

Spoon large dollops of the cream cheese mixture over the brownie layer, spacing evenly. Use a spoon to swirl/marbleize the topping. Sprinkle with the almonds if using.

Bake in preheated oven for about 30 to 35 minutes, or until brownie appears set but a toothpick inserted in the center will have wet crumbs clinging to it.

Cool completely, then cut into 24 squares.

Makes one 9-inch-square cake, serving 8 to 10

1 ½ cups boiling water

1 cup rolled oats

1 cup packed brown sugar

1 cup granulated sugar

½ cup vegetable oil

1 ½ cups flour

1 teaspoon cinnamon

1 teaspoon baking soda

½ teaspoon salt

Topping

8 tablespoons (1 stick) butter

1 cup packed brown sugar

½ cup milk

1 cup (3 ounces) Angel Flake-style coconut

1 teaspoon vanilla extract

Professional golfer Jack Nicklaus is the all-time leader in major tournament wins, and has been voted PGA Player of the Year five times. His wife, Barbara Nicklaus, keeps up just fine with her own golf titles: First Lady of Golf and the Ambassador of Golf.

JACK & BARBARA NICKLAUS
OATMEAL CAKE

Scotland has given the world wonderful baked goods, as well as the wonderful game of golf. In addition to its famous shortbread and scones, Scottish cuisine makes extensive use of oats, as in this homespun oatmeal cake.

To make the cake: Preheat oven to 350°F. Grease and flour a 9-inch square pan.

Pour measured boiling water over oats and let sit.

In a large bowl, combine the brown and granulated sugars with oil and mix well. In a small bowl, mix together the flour, cinnamon, baking soda, and salt, then add to sugar mixture. Add oat mixture and stir well.

Scrape batter into prepared pan, and rap pan on counter to release any bubbles. Bake in preheated oven for 35 to 40 minutes, or until cake tests done.

To make the topping: In a saucepan, combine the butter, brown sugar, and milk; bring to a boil and boil for 5 minutes.

Add the coconut and vanilla. Prick top of cake with a fork and pour topping over hot cake. Let cool.

Serve directly from the pan.

THINGS YOU SHOULD KNOW

Cooking is an art, and many factors affect the outcome of a dish. Oven temperatures and burner heats vary, and ingredients from different parts of the country differ as well. Use your best judgment when making the recipes in this book.

- Butter is salted unless otherwise noted.

- Flour is all-purpose unless otherwise noted.

- Ginger is peeled unless otherwise noted.

- Garlic, onions, and carrots are peeled unless otherwise noted.

To make lemon or other citrus zest: Zest is the outer peel of citrus fruit—with no white pith. You can use a fine zesting tool that makes long, very thin, pretty strands, or you can peel off the zest with an ordinary potato peeler, being sure not to get any white pith, and then cut it in very, very thin, long strips or mince it.

To toast nuts: Place the nuts on a rimmed baking sheet and toast in preheated 350°F oven for about 10 minutes, or until golden. Nuts can also be toasted in an ungreased pan or skillet over medium heat, stirring frequently.

Raw eggs, raw fish, and raw shellfish are not recommended for pregnant women, children, the elderly, or anyone with immune deficiencies.

INDEX

A

Agassi, Andre, 74
Allen, Paul G., 78
Amos, Tori, 132-133
Anastacia, 148
Aoki, Rocky H., 44, 131
Appetizers
    chicken wings marinara, 14
    lamb-stuffed vine leaves, 18
    rosemary Parmesan puffs, 28
    shrimp cocktail, 17
    tuna pizza, 22
    wontons in hot-and-sour chili sauce, 26
Apple pie, 148
Armintrout, Libby Gates, 8-9, 52

B

Bacon strips, crispy brown-sugared, 140
Balsamic glaze, 43
Banana nut bread, 124
Bastianich, Lidia, 70, 152-153
Beans, baked, 130
Beef
    dump chili, 111
    filet de boeuf Béarnaise, 68
    pot roast, classic, with caramelized onion gravy, 101
    rib steaks, grilled, with panzanella, 71
    skirt steak, marinated, 56
    steak, bronzed, with gingersnap gravy, 64
    Stroganoff, 108
Benihana fried rice, 131
Benihana salad dressing, 44
Bento box, 158
Bergen, Candice, 60-61
Beverages
    green juice, 24
    mandarin star, 21
    watermelon twist, 31
Black, Clint, 102-103
Blackberry, warm, whipped egg custard, 161

Bloomberg, Michael R., 130
Borscht, Ukrainian, 46
Bread
    banana nut, 124
    cornbread with honey glaze, 136
Brosnan, Pierce, 94-95
Brownies, raspberry cream cheese, 162

C

Cabbage, stuffed, Hungarian, 110
Cake, oatmeal, 163
Cannon, Dyan, 151
Casey, Kathy, 21, 28
Cheesecake, pineapple, with macadamia nut crust, 157
Chicken
    & dumplings, 115
    gumbo, 35
    jambalaya, 79
    King Ranch, 107
    lemon, 66
    Mexican dinner, 102
    piccata with pine nuts and capers, 58
    salad, almond, 106
    salad, tropical, 36
    sauerkraut, 112
    Sauterne, 78
    soup, noodle, 53
    wings marinara, 14
Chili, dump, 111
Chocolate
    mousse parfaits, 151
    soufflés, 158
Chowder, clam, 52
Choy, Sam, 157
Clam chowder, 52
Clinton, Chelsea, 128
Connick, Harry, Jr., 79
Cooper, Alice, 106
Cooper, Sheryl, 106
Corn, scallop, tomato salad, 41

Cornbread with honey glaze, 136

Couric, Katie, 66

Crab

    gumbo, 35

    seafood pasta, 82

Cranberry relish, red wine, 74

Crawfish, seafood pasta, 82

Curry, Ann, 86-87

Curry, Mark, 136

Custard, whipped egg, warm blackberry, 161

D

Danza, Tony, 118

Dion, Celine, 18-19

Douglas, Tom, 71, 154

Dutch babies, 139

E

Eisner, Michael, 93

English, Todd, 48-49

Evert, Chris, 36-37

F

Faggots & mushy peas with mint, 116

Fennel oil, 43

Fennel, shaved, salad of Black Mission figs,
    roasted sweet peppers, 42

Fennel, watermelon & black olive salad with
    feta cheese, 48

Figs, Black Mission, salad, with roasted sweet
    peppers and shaved fennel, 42-43

G

Gates, Bill, 52

Graf, Stefanie, 74

Grant, Amy, 124-125

Grapes, rustic roasted pears &, 152

Gumbo, Janet Hill's, 35

H

Ham, gumbo, 35

Hamilton, Scott, 120-121

Hamm, Mia, 135

Hartman-Black, Lisa, 102-103

Henderson, Florence, 58

Hill, Grant, 34-35

Hill, Janet, 35

Hurley, Elizabeth, 104-105

I

Ice cream, sesame, 158

Il Ristorante di Giorgio Baldi, 94

J

Jambalaya, 79

Joel, Billy, 56

Jones, Quincy, 112

Jones, Tom, 116-117

Juice, green, 24

K

Karan, Donna, 24

Keller, Thomas, 42-43

Kerr, Graham, 38, 161

Kors, Michael, 41

Kournikova, Anna, 46-47

Kugel, noodle, 142

L

Lagasse, Emeril, 65, 73

Lajaunie, Chef Philippe, 68

Lamb

    chops, seared, with rosemary and
    mint sauce, 70

    shepherd's pie, 104

    stuffed vine leaves, 18

Lauder, Evelyn, 50

Leno, Jay, 14-15

Lobster ravioli with tomato tarragon
    cream sauce, 92

Lucci, Susan, 84

Lukins, Sheila, 17, 76

Lunden, Joan, 89

M

Macaroni & cheese, baked, 96

Mandarin star, 21

Mathies, Chef John, 100-101

Matsuhisa, Nobuyuki, 158

McGrady, Tracy, 90-91

McGraw, Dr. Phil, 143

McGraw, Tim, 115

Meatballs, spaghetti &, 84

Mexican dinner, 102

Mickelson, Phil, 92

Minnie Mouse, 93

Morimoto, Masaharu, 22

Mourning, Alonzo, 147

N

Nicklaus, Barbara, 163

Nicklaus, Jack, 163

Noodle kugel, 142

P

Palmer, Arnold, 140

Parfaits, chocolate mousse, 151

Pasta

lobster ravioli with tomato tarragon cream sauce, 92

macaroni & cheese, baked, 96

penne al funghi porcini, 94

puttanesca, 86

seafood, 82

smoked salmon linguine, 90

spaghetti & meatballs, 84

vegetable, 93

Pataki, Libby, 110

Pears, rustic roasted, & grapes, 152

Peppers, roasted, 43

Pickford, Chef Duncan, 132

Pie

apple, 148

sweet potato, 147

Pineapple cheesecake with macadamia nut crust, 157

Pizza, tuna, 22

Pompano with citrus crust and grapefruit butter sauce, 73

Porcini, penne al funghi, 94

Pork

faggots & mushy peas with mint, 116

wontons in hot-and-sour chili sauce, 26

Pot roast, classic, with caramelized onion gravy, 101

Potatoes, mashed, rosemary, 143

Preston, Kelly, 108

Prudhomme, Paul, 64

Puffs, rosemary Parmesan, 28

R

Rae's noodle kugel, 142

Rascal Flatts, 53

Raspberry cream cheese brownies, 162

Rice, fried, 131

Risotto, pumpkin & sage, with mushroom and pea ragout, 89

Rivers, Joan, 126

Roddick, Andy, 68

Romano, Ray, 162

Rosemary Parmesan puffs, 28

S

Salad

almond chicken, 106

chicken, tropical, 36

fennel, watermelon & black olive, with feta cheese, 48

figs, Black Mission, with roasted sweet peppers and shaved fennel, 42-43

scallop, corn, tomato, 41

shrimp, 50

Salad dressing, Benihana, 44

Salmon
  burgers, 60
  smoked, linguine, 90
  wild, seared, with summer fruit salsa, 62
Sandwich
  heirloom tomato, with Gorgonzola aioli
    on focaccia, 118
  tuna, 120
Sauce
  Béarnaise, 68
  tomato tarragon cream, 92
Sauerkraut, chicken, 112
Sausage
  gumbo, 35
  jambalaya, 79
Scallop corn tomato salad, 41
Schultz, Howard, 142
Seafood pasta, 82
Shepherd's pie, 104
Shortcakes, strawberry cornmeal, 154
Shrimp
  cocktail, 17
  gumbo, 35
  salad, 50
  seafood pasta, 82
Sills, Beverly, 139
Skerritt, Tom, 62-63
Smith, Liz, 31
Soup
  borscht, Ukrainian, 46
  chicken noodle, 53
  clam chowder, 52
  gumbo, 35
  vegetable, Mediterranean, 38
Spaghetti & meatballs, 84
Spears, Britney, 82
Spears, Lynne, 82
Steak
  marinated skirt, 56
  rib, grilled, with panzanella, 71
  tenderloin, with Béarnaise sauce, 68

  tenderloin, bronzed, with gingersnap gravy, 64
Strait, George, 107
Strawberry cornmeal shortcakes, 154
Sweet potato
  casserole, 128
  coconut mashed, 65
  pie, 147
Swordfish Provençal, 76

T
Toast, 126
Tomato
  heirloom, sandwich with Gorgonzola aioli on
    focaccia, 118
  scallop corn, salad, 41
Tuna
  pizza, 22
  sandwich, 120
Turkey, herb roast, with red wine cranberry
  relish, 74
Turnips, glazed, 132

V
Veal shanks braised with rum over coconut
  mashed sweet potatoes, 65
Vegetable, soup, Mediterranean, 38
Vegetables, grilled summer, 135
Vinaigrette, lemon thyme, 135
Vodka, mandarin star, 21

W
Wariner, Steve, 96
Watermelon, fennel, & black olive salad, 48
Watermelon twist, 31
Williams, Robin, 100-101
Williams, Venus, 111
Wontons in hot-and-sour chili sauce, 26

Y
Yan, Martin, 26

BENEFICIARIES

MARSHA RIVKIN CENTER FOR OVARIAN CANCER RESEARCH

Founded in 1996 by prominent oncologist Dr. Saul Rivkin and his five daughters in memory of his wife, who passed away after a long battle with ovarian cancer, the Marsha Rivkin Center works closely with its renowned partners: Swedish Medical Center, the region's most extensive cancer-treatment facility, which has been treating cancer patients for more than 80 years; and Fred Hutchinson Cancer Research Center, internationally recognized for its pioneering research.

The Marsha Rivkin Center is dedicated to saving lives and reducing suffering through improved treatment, early detection, and prevention of ovarian cancer. Research funding from the Marsha Rivkin Center has provided the momentum to turn ovarian cancer pilot studies into nationally funded research initiatives—including a Department of Defense New Investigator Award and a $12 million National Institutes of Health Specialized Program in Research Excellence.

For more information, please call (800) 328-1124 or visit www.marsharivkin.org.

Marsha Rivkin Center for Ovarian Cancer Research
1221 Madison St., Suite 1401
Seattle, WA 98104

THE BREAST CANCER RESEARCH FOUNDATION

Founded in 1993 by Evelyn H. Lauder, The Breast Cancer Research Foundation is dedicated to the belief that through innovative clinical and genetic research, breast cancer can be prevented and a cure can be found in our lifetime. The brilliant minds of our researchers —"the best brain trust in the country, perhaps the world," according to Michael Zinner, MD at Harvard—are breaking new frontiers on topics such as genetic factors, vaccines, clinical trials, the relationship of dietary and environmental factors to breast cancer, state-of-the-art detection technology, breast cancer in African-American and Latino communities and in young women, and psycho-social implications of breast-cancer diagnosis and treatment.

A minimum of 85 cents of every dollar donated to the Foundation goes directly to research and public-awareness programs. The Foundation received four stars (the highest possible rating) from Charity Navigator and an "A" from the American Institute of Philanthropy.

For more information, please call 1.866.FIND.A.CURE (toll-free) or visit www.bcrfcure.org.

The Breast Cancer Research Foundation
654 Madison Avenue, Suite 1209
New York, New York 10021

SPECIAL THANKS

Cookbook Committee
Eric Bensussen
Gloria Bensussen (Chair)
Karen Gamoran
Mimi Gan
Craig Gilbert
Evelyn H. Lauder
Chuck Lytle
Scott Oki
Lynne Spears
Bonnie Towne

Marsha Rivkin Center
Jocelyn Moore
Saul Rivkin, MD

Breast Cancer Research Foundation
Pat Altman
Myra Biblowit
Anna Deluca
Robbie Finke

The Red Army Creative
Diana Fryc
Colleen Gray
Shandy Henderson
Kong Lu
Jenn Morey
Jill Sato
Gary Wong

Studio 3
David Bell
Sheri Hauser
Chris Jackson
Dana Laurent
Dennis Wise

Documentary Media
Petyr Beck
Barry Provorse

Kathy Casey Food Studios
John Casey
Liv Fagerholm
Mindy Hankins
Ann Manly
Antonette Rudge

Additional Acknowledgments
Melissa Bedolis
Jackie Bezos
Susan Callahan
David Chessnoff
Darlene Daggett
Keven Davis
Mary Dixon
Audrey D'Onofrio
Candice Douglas
Friesens Corporation
Richard Galanti
Libby Gates Armintrout
Roblee Harris
Alexandra Kau
Arthur Klebanoff
KNCB Dave
Don Listwin
John McMahon
Paul Murphy
Melissa Rivkin
Kari Schwartz
Stuart Sloan
Traecy Smith
Margaret Stewart
The StrataGem Group

THE
BRITNEY
SPEARS
FOUNDATION

*Special thanks to the
Britney Spears Foundation
for helping make this
book a reality*

Star Palate Team

Front Row: Tami Agassi, Gloria Bensussen, Eric Bensussen, Kathy Casey (standing), Kong Lu, Mimi Gan, Jim Bianco. Candice Douglas

Back Row: Craig Gilbert, Barry Provorse (standing), Jocelyn Moore (standing), Christine Boutée, Gary Wong (standing), Ann Manly, Sheri Hauser, Dana Laurent (standing), Diana Fryc (standing), David Bell, Christine Jackson, Bonnie Towne

(Not all team members are pictured)

SPECIAL SPONSOR

This cookbook would not have been possible without the generous funding provided by Cell Therapeutics, Inc., a biopharmaceutical company focused on developing therapies that combat cancer without compromising patient quality of life. For more information, please visit www.cticseattle.com.

Making cancer more treatable®

CREDITS

All food photography by David Bell, Studio 3, food styling by Christine Jackson except where otherwise noted.

Front Cover
Britney Spears photo by Mary Ellen Matthews
Andre Agassi photo by John Russell

5	Photos by Marc Carter and Tami Agassi
10-11	Photos by Marc Carter and Tami Agassi
24	Photo by Jennifer Livingston/CPI
26	Photo by Geoff George
	Recipe originally from *Martin Yan's Chinatown Cooking*, ©2002, A La Carte
34	Photo by Lasting Impressions by Ellyn
37	Photo by Steve Grubman
42-43	Photo by Deborah Jones
	Recipe originally from *The French Laundry Cookbook*, ©2000, Artisan
44	Photo by Hiroshi Abe
	Recipe originally from www.benihana.com
47	Photo by Bill Ling
48	Recipe originally from www.toddenglish.com
52	Photo by Richard Brown
53	Photo by David Johnson
56	Photo by Patrick Demarchelier
61	Photo by Thomas Mangieri
63	Photo by Dennis Wise/©2004 Studio 3, Inc.
64	Recipe ©2000 by Paul Prudhomme
65	Photo by Steven Freeman
68	Photo by Michael Baz
	Recipe courtesy of Chef Philippe Lajaunie, Les Halles Restaurant, New York
75	Photo by John Russell
82	Photo by Mark Liddell
87	Photo by Jayne Wexler
89	Photo by Andrew Eccles
89	Recipe originally from *Growing Up Healthy: A Complete Guide to Childhood Nutrition and Well-Being, Birth Through Adolescence*, by Joan Lunden and Myron Winick, ©2004, Atria Books
94	Recipe courtesy of Chef Giorgio Baldi, Il Ristorante di Giorgio Baldi, Santa Monica
95	Photo by Greg Gorman
96	Photo by Jim McGuire
101	Recipe courtesy of Chef John Mathies
105	Photo by Antoine Verglas
111	Photo by Charles William Bush
115	Photo by Marina Chavez
125	Photo by Sam Jones
130	Photo by Ed Reed
131	Recipe originally from www.benihana.com
132	Recipe and photo courtesy of Chef Duncan Pickford
133	Photo by Kurt Mertus
139	Photo by Martha Swope Associates/Carol Rosegg
142	Photos courtesy of Howard Schultz
143	Recipe reprinted with permission from *The Ultimate Weight Solution Cookbook*, by Dr. Phil McGraw, ©2004, Free Press
153	Photo by Mario Novak Photography
154	Photo by Robin Layton
158	Photo by Sam Stia
164	Photo by Tami Agassi
174	Photo by Dennis Wise/©2004 Studio 3

Back Cover
Tim McGraw photo by Marina Chavez
Elizabeth Hurley photo by Antoine Verglas
Grant Hill photo by Lasting Impressions by Ellyn
Emeril Lagasse photo by Steven Freeman

Back Flap
Photo by Rosanne Olson